CHEYENNE FRONTIER DAYS™ THE FIRST 100 YEARS

A Pictorial History

©1996, Cheyenne Newspapers, Inc.
ALL RIGHTS RESERVED. No part of this publication may be reproduced, stored in a retrieval system, or transmitted by any means, electronic, mechanical, photocopying, recording, or otherwise, without the prior written permission of the publisher and the copyright holder.
ISBN 0-9652275-0-2

A note of thanks

We at the Wyoming Tribune-Eagle would like to thank our many readers who made this book possible by submitting their photos and memorabilia from Cheyenne Frontier Days™. Hundreds of photos, clippings, postcards and other souvenirs were submitted, providing a challenging task for Shirley Flynn and Randy Wagner, our photo selection and design consultants.

We would also like to recognize the efforts of several Wyoming Tribune-Eagle employees, including:

Scott Walker, advertising director, who had the idea for this book and served as project coordinator.

Katy Hinckley, promotions manager, who coordinated promotion of the book and designed its cover.

Gloria Anderson, administrative secretary, who received and managed all the materials submitted and handled book orders.

Dick Moody, production director, and the Graphics and Commerical Printing staffs, who composed and printed the book.

Thanks, also, to the many other Wyoming Tribune-Eagle employees who were involved with this project.

Finally, as we enjoy this year's 100th annual celebration of Cheyenne Frontier Days™, we all owe a debt of gratitude to Colonel Edward Archibald Slack, credited by many as being the "father" of this grand festival of the Old West. Colonel Slack, owner of the Cheyenne Daily Sun-Leader, a predecessor of today's Wyoming Tribune-Eagle, was the first booster and a co-founder of what is now Cheyenne Frontier Days™. Without Colonel Slack's early moral and financial support and the promotion of the event he provided through his newspaper, Cheyenne Frontier Days™ might never have begun. He would be proud to see that Cheyenne's original one-day celebration of its frontier heritage has grown into a 10-day western extravaganza known worldwide as the "Daddy of 'em All®."

L. Michael McCraken
President & Publisher
Wyoming Tribune-Eagle

Acknowledgements

TABLE OF CONTENTS

Chapter 1	Page 1	RODEO
Chapter 2	Page 28	COWBOYS AND COWGIRLS
Chapter 3	Page 44	PARADES
Chapter 4	Page 64	PEOPLE
Chapter 5	Page 80	PARTIES, PLACES AND PLAYTIME
Chapter 6	Page 104	VOLUNTEERS
Chapter 7	Page 151	CONTRIBUTORS

This collection of Cheyenne Frontier Days™ photographs is indeed something special.

To create this book, subscribers and readers of the Wyoming Tribune-Eagle were invited to submit their photographs of Cheyenne Frontier Days™. From scrapbooks, dens, basements and attics came hundreds of images, each of which means something to someone - each important enough to have been saved for years, decades or generations.

This is not a museum collection, nor is it a complete history of the world's largest outdoor rodeo. Rather, it is a series of brief glimpses into the history of the nation's greatest and longest-running western celebration - an event started and nurtured by Colonel Edward Archibald Slack.

Slack was a young newspaperman when he came to Cheyenne in 1876 and purchased a local newspaper that was a predecessor of today's Wyoming Tribune-Eagle.

Credited by many as being the "father" of Cheyenne Frontier Days™, Slack saw the value in starting a local rodeo show to call attention to Cheyenne after he was visited by a passenger agent for the Union Pacific Railroad. The agent wanted to promote excursion rides from Denver to towns along the rail line and encouraged leaders of the various communities to create local festivals to help draw visitors.

The first booster and a co-founder of what is now Cheyenne Frontier Days™, Slack solicited financial and volunteer support for the event from other local business owners. He used his newspaper, the Cheyenne Daily Sun-Leader, to promote the idea and to suggest the name "Frontier Day" for the first one-day celebration, held September 23, 1897.

Slack remained a civic leader and a staunch promoter of the celebration until his death in 1907 at age 65. His unwavering support helped lay the foundation for today's success and popularity of Cheyenne Frontier Days™.

What began as a one-day amateur event showcasing the talents of some rough and tumble cowpokes from local ranches has grown into a 10-day western extravaganza known worldwide. The celebration brings hundreds of thousands of visitors to Cheyenne each July and has an economic impact on the community of many millions of dollars.

Since the days when Slack's creation first took shape, people have been collecting snapshots and postcards of the event.

Col. E.A. Slack

The photos in this book are presented as they were received. The scratches, tears, stains, faded images and thumbtack holes are there for all to see, as are the inscriptions on many of the pictures. No attempt was made to improve or alter any images.

Most of the photographs are being publicly presented here for the first time. Only a few, those needed to fill the gaps in the 100-year Cheyenne Frontier Days™ story, will be recognized by folks who have visited museum and gallery displays or studied other books on the history of the event.

The Wyoming Tribune-Eagle is proud to be a part of the rich history of Cheyenne Frontier Days™, and we thank the hundreds of subscribers and readers who took the time to dig through family memorabilia so they could share these images with us.

Introduction

THE RODEO

RODEO! The word conjures up many things, but always at its center is the competition among cowboys and the struggle of man against animal. Rodeo as a sport grew from the working cowhand's pride in his skills . . . and his bragging about it! Competitions took place in ranch corrals among the 'hands of an outfit; then, the cowboys at one ranch pitted themselves against those from another. About 1885, the colorful cowboys and their exciting sport hit the road with Wild West shows.

From the first contest here in 1897, the Frontier Committee provided the best, or worst, stock on which the determined cowboy could test himself; ropers and 'doggers brought their own superbly trained mounts. Rain or shine, the events followed one another in the huge arena fostered by fair rules and generous prizes.

Saddle bronc riding, always the cornerstone of competition, and the wild horse race have bucked along every year since 1897. Steer roping was scheduled the first year but not held. Bulldogging evolved after 1904 and was sanctioned in 1914. Amateur bucking was added to the program in 1911, and calf roping in 1920. It was not until 1936 that bareback bronc riding and bull riding were officially counted. Chuck wagon racing thundered down from the north in 1952.

Today, the cowboy competitor, the contractor with the stock and the Frontier Committee partner to create the world's largest outdoor rodeo, our "Daddy of 'em All."

Both the bucking bronco and the rider, Cliff Helms, showed fine form, c. 1935.

Ramona Merritt stood on the back of the loaded pickup to check the gear and say goodbye as her father, King, left for a rodeo.

SADDLE

Before the days of chutes, the bronco was snubbed to another horse, then the cowboy climbed aboard. Each ride was a complete rodeo!

Tex Crockett on South Dakota. R.R. Doubleday did a brisk business selling post cards made from his photographs. He took photographs each afternoon and had the post cards ready for sale by nightfall.

Dolf Aber on Quicksilver. Aber, a Sheridan, Wyoming cowboy, won bronc riding in 1939.

BRONCS

Cowboys and cowgirls, often 1,000 strong, galloped through a Grand Entry in the early days.

C.B. Irwin won steer roping in 1906. This photograph, by J.E. Stimson, was made into a post card. These cards are now prized collector items.

Old Steamboat bucked here from 1903 to 1914. He was at his peak in 1908.

Dave Whyte, a Cheyenne man, won first money on "Texico" in 1923.

Another photographer is taking a picture of this classic ride.

Yakima Canutt rodeoed in the early 1920s, then went to Hollywood as a stuntman and stock contractor for the movies. His wife, Kitty, traveled on the rodeo circuit with him.

Five Minutes to Midnight bucked here from 1929 to 1945.

Skeeter Thurston rode Rusty in the finals, 1986. He got his start in rodeo by winning Rookie Bronc Riding in 1982. Rusty always gave a good, or bad, ride, depending on your perspective.

GREAT

HORSES

 Angel Sings, a well-known bucker, gave Mike Anderson a great ride in 1982.

Four times World Champion Saddle Bronc Rider Brad Gjermundson teamed up with Bobby Joe Skoal for a trip to the pay window in 1990. Gjermundson also won here in 1984.

WILD HORSE RACE

8510. Cowboy Race with Wild Bronchos, Frontier Day, Cheyenne, Wyo.

🌵 "Cowboys race with wild broncos."
The wild horse race has been held every year for a century.

🌵 After saddling the wild one, the rider must make it around the track; a teammate nearby can help get things started.

Team members calm a wild one today just as they did 100 years ago.

STEER WRESTLING

Dick Truitt came from Stonewall, Oklahoma, to win steer wrestling in 1936.

Steer wrestling, or bull dogging, was introduced by Will Pickett in 1904. This unidentified cowboy shows good form.

Timers watch the action from the stand over Chute 9, c. 1940.

12

Jock Dalton, grandson of the legendary King Merritt, ropes steers in the best family tradition. Dalton is on his favorite horse, Red.

STEER

Buzz Bradley, a native son, practiced his roping skills as a member of the Cheyenne Roping Club.

Roy Cooper captured the title of All Around Champion here in 1989 and 1993. Steer roping is his specialty.

ROPING

Bucky Hefner caught the steer roping buckle in 1995. The roper's horse gets extra grain for a job well done.

14

👢 The maverick branding contest was an early version of calf roping. Charles Irwin sits on the horse in the center, Charles Carey (in light pants) is walking, and the man on the horse at right is Howard Marsh. A photographer is moving into the action.

CALF

👢 This photograph of Dee Burk was taken in 1942, during the first show of World War II years.

Don McLaughlin called Ft. Worth, Texas, his home when he won the All Around title in both 1959 and 1960. In 1983, when this photograph was taken, he was roping on the senior circuit; he won the buckle here in 1991.

ROPING

Tom Ferguson captured All Around honors in 1976. The winner must win money in two events. This photo was taken in 1994.

16

Paul Carney won bareback bronc riding in 1937. The year after that the sport became a recognized event at Frontier Days.

BAREBACK BRONC RIDING

 Joe Alexander won bareback riding here in 1973, 1974 and 1976. He hailed from Cora, Wyoming, during the years he competed here.

Many said this ride by Bruce Ford on Khadafy in 1989 was the best they had ever seen.

Chris LeDoux is best known now as a country/western entertainer. His family lived here in the 1960s; he attended Cheyenne High School and fell in love with rodeo.

Paul Wiederholt rode the famous bull 777 in 1981.

Photographer Randy Wagner caught Lane Frost in this ride in 1988.

THE BULLS AND BULL RIDERS

David Gaither climbed on Mr. T, a dream-breaker, in 1988.

👢 Ty Murray was All Around champion in 1990 and won the saddle bronc buckle in 1993.

👢 Tuff Hedeman earned a score of 83 during the first go around in 1995. He went on to win the event.

20

🤠 The crowd cheers and stomps as 16 thoroughbred horses, four wagons and drivers, and eight outriders plunge around the first turn...

THUNDER FROM THE NORTH

🤠

...and hurtle around the half-mile track to the finish line.

Carefully curried, well fed and alert, the horses of Buddy Bensmiller patiently wait for the next race. Home is Dewberry, Alberta, Canada.

Although crumpled from use, this 1954 photograph shows the dust and scramble of chuckwagon racing.

Out West Photos, one of several companies engaged in the trade, printed this photograph as a post card in 1940.

KIDS & CALVES

A rollicking ride.

For calf riding, a movable chute was set up on the track to bring the action closer to the grandstands.

Jonnie Jonckowski, a pretty blonde with plenty of grit, made exhibition rides in 1988 and 1989.

Melanie Dalton, showing good form, won first place riding her horse, Merthiolate, in 1970.

THE COWGIRLS

Nancy Hemming rode in the wild horse race. A good rider, she was the first woman to enter the event in many years.

👢 The Serpentine drill started the rodeo with a splash of color and a dash of action in the 1960s.

THE BIG

🥾 The Dinner Bell Derby. Kept from their mothers for a day, hungry colts dash to dinner during the Mare and Colt Race.

SHOW

🥾 Panoramas were taken almost every year until the mid-1940s. They form a passing parade of cowboys, horses, Indians and spectators over the years.

Billy Cramer pushed up the brim of his hat and arranged all his lariats for his formal portrait in 1899 when he won bronc riding.

COWBOYS AND COWGIRLS

After the civil war a new breed of men came up the cattle trails from Texas. Mounted on barely-broke horses, they trailed cattle along the endless route. To ease the tedium and quiet the herds at night, they sang, "Whoop-ee-ti-yi-o get along little doggies, you know that Wyoming will be your new home."

To survive, the man was tough and resourceful. His word was bond; he protected women, valued friendships, and he shot straight. He said he could rope and ride better than any other man, and he was proud of it. Danger lurked over every hill, and at every creek crossing. He was brave. The Eastern press couldn't get enough of his exploits.

Buffalo Bill took him on Grand Tours with his Wild West Show and Congress of Roughriders of the World. A myth grew around our newly minted hero. He emerged a "cowboy" ready to perform and compete for prizes. His specialized clothing, a 10-gallon hat, heeled boots, wooly chaps, and a neckerchief, was his hallmark.

Every ranch hand hankered to join the ranks of the rodeo cowboy. For the first Frontier Days, cowboys came from a 50-mile radius riding their best mounts and trailing a bucker. Prize money awaited the best riders and ropers in ol' Cheyenne, the BIG one. A win here certified that he was the champion of the world!

Early in the century a bevy of hard-riding women joined the rodeo competition. They, too, wanted the glory of winning at Cheyenne. In satins, silks and big hats, they entertained the crowds while they rode for prizes.

After a century, the lore of the cowboy of old and the lure of winning at "the Daddy," still runs deep. Over 1,100 hopefuls pay their entry fee; each knows he has a chance at the buckle that proclaims him champion at Cheyenne Frontier Days.

Friends: Ike Rude and King Merritt, c. 1930.

Helen Bowen won the ladies' steer roping contest, 1914.

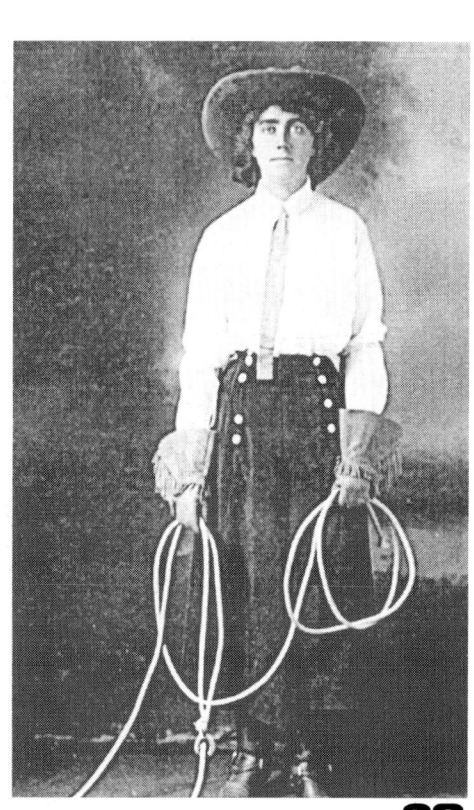

Otto Plaga, Gill Jacobsen, Billy Frazier and an unidentified companion lined up for a photograph in 1902 or 1903.

Jack Elliot, Floyd Carroll, Jesse Coats and Don Thompson stand ready to compete, 1907. Carroll went on to be a veterinarian and Elliot a stock contractor.

The angora chaps were retired, but the cowboys still enjoyed Frontier Days in 1915. Note the bow ties sported by the two on the left.

By 1929 the cowboys dressed to work.

CHANGING STYLES

In the mid-1950s the rodeo cowboys still wore big hats, boots, and grins.

30

Photographer J.E. Stimson caught bronc rider Goldie St. Clair riding a rough one, c. 1910.

Prairie Rose Henderson entered bronc riding, relay races and trick riding. She was famous for her flamboyant outfits.

"On my pony from old Cheyenne." This old post card shows unidentified riders with torches in front of the old Congregational Church at 19th Street and Capitol Avenue. It is part of a parking lot today.

👢 Donna Card Glover was typical of the pretty cowgirls of the 1920s.

Bonnie Grey traveled the rodeo circuit during the 1920s. On King Tut, a huge horse, she jumped over a touring car.

👢 Mabel Strickland won bronc riding in 1923, and the <u>Denver Post Ladies Relay Race</u> in 1922 and 1923.

THE LADIES

👢 Cowgirl contestants, 1924, turned in their split skirts for jodhpurs. From the left: Bea Kirnan, Rose Smith, Mabel Strickland, Fox Hastings, Ruth Roach and Florence Hughes.

32

Ramona Merritt, daughter of King, rode in the flat races popular in the 1940s.

Wilma Moncrief wore a ballet costume while trick riding in 1926. A newspaper columnist chided, "Wilma, have you no chaps?"

Trick rider Juanita Grey struts her stuff. Always a popular competition, trick riding was dropped as an event after 1940.

Turk Greenough at seven stood ready for action. He won saddle bronc riding in 1933, 1935 and 1936.

YOUNGSTERS

Dewey Lee David was the world's youngest trick rider at six.

Dewey Lee David rode his well-trained horse, Skippy, in 1942.

34

THE TURTLES

Carl Arnold called Buckeye, Arizona, home. He won steer roping here in 1930, 1945 and 1947. He then worked many years as "boss" of Chute 9.

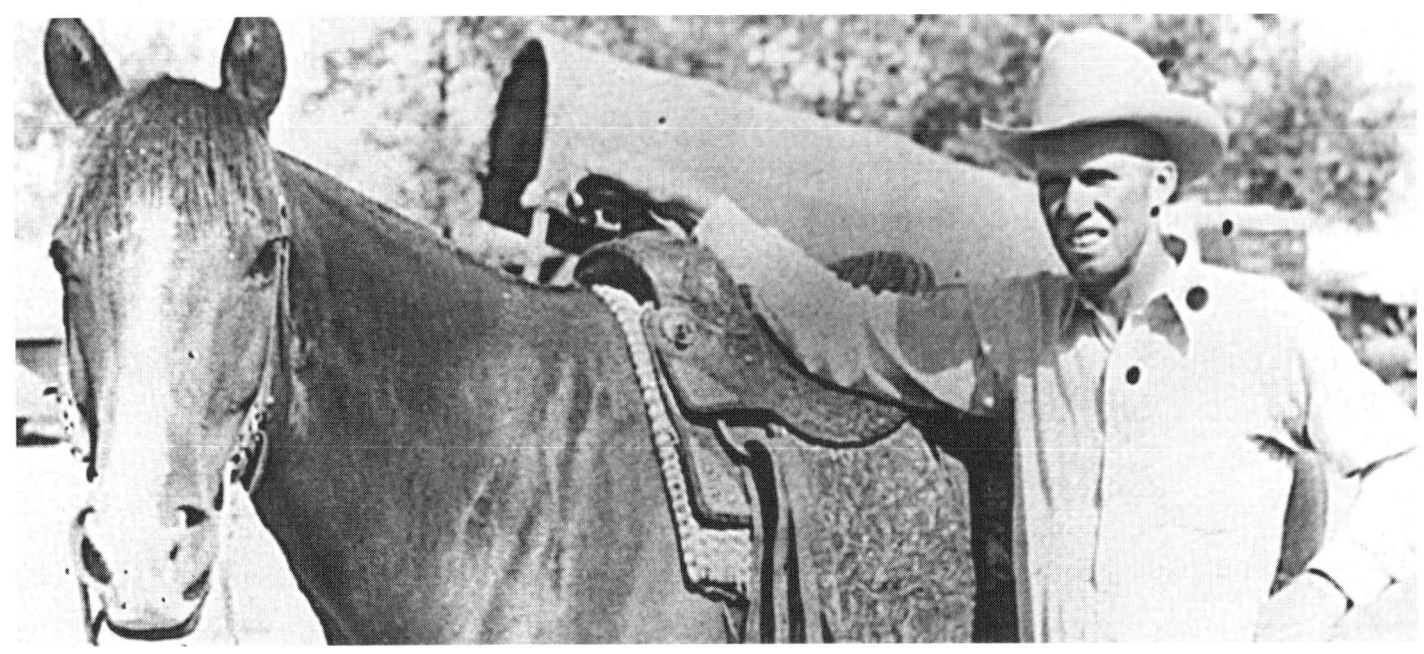

King Merritt raised fine horses along with a fine family of rodeo hands. He stands with his famed roping horse, Bullet.

The Cowboys Turtle Association held their 1942 meeting at the Elks Club. Note the businesses in the background: The Bluebird, the Capitol Garage, the Elks Home and the Tribune-Eagle Building.

GETTING READY

Pretty girls, called Buckle Bunnies, decorate the corral areas.

A place of prayer and preparation for the cowboy, the Ready Room, also becomes an office, a storehouse for gear and a meeting hall during the rodeo.

Buddy Bensmiller, from Dewberry, Alberta, Canada, brushes his lead horse before a chuckwagon race, 1995.

Brad Goodrich, roper, checked his answering service hourly in 1995.

The Cowboy Ready Room. One cowboy found a secluded corner to store his gear during the rodeo.

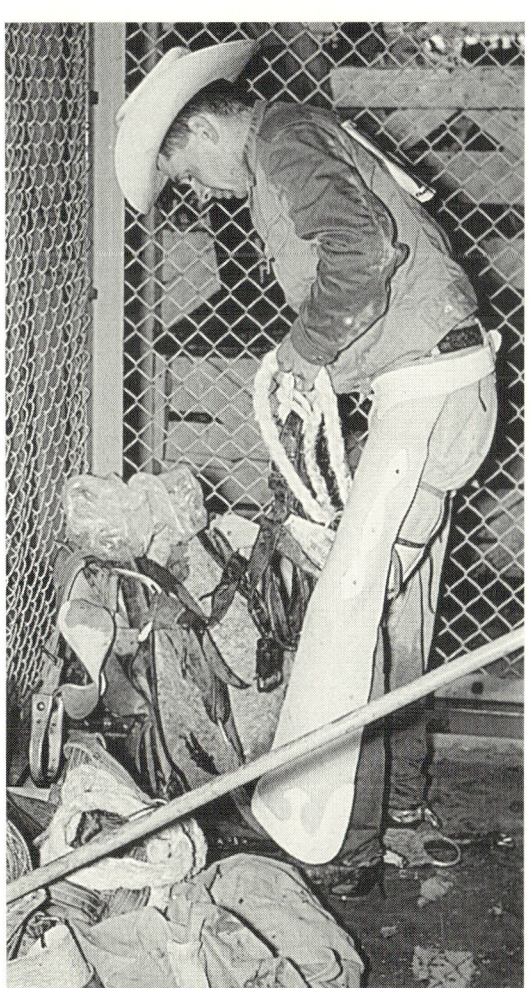

 Rodeo legend Jim Shoulders and Dick Picket take a break from the rodeo action. Shoulders won honors in bull and bareback riding; Picket served as CFD Chairman in 1980 and 1981.

The 1963 lineup of champions. Standing: Ralph Maynard, Tex Martin, Bob Wagner, Jim Shoulders, Ronnie Sewalt, Miss Frontier Suzanne Hanes, Lady-In-Waiting Susan Dubois, Shoat Webster, Neil Love, and Bill Greenwood. Front row with The Denver Post trophy saddle: wild horse race winners Lee Wilson, Larry Benson and Frank Baber.

THE GOOD OL' BOYS AND GIRLS

 Stock contractor Verne Elliott, July 28, 1951, surveys the scene!

Kaycee, Wyoming, residents Chris LeDoux and Larry Sandvick (bareback rider) get together for a few laughs in 1995.

Men at work: Bobby Romer, Quail Dobbs in the barrel and Wick Peth stand ready to rescue Jim Ketter.

SEND IN THE CLOWNS

 Bobby Romer signed autographs for his fans, young and old.

With rapt attention, Rick Chapman and Dwayne Hargo watch Quinten Lowery to ensure his safety, 1984.

Quail Dobbs named his pet pig Hilary and his car Apollo. Hilary only squeeled, but the car roared, belched smoke and blasted off.

Wilbur Plaugher, rodeo clown and animal trainer, could talk to his lovingly-tended animals.

PARADES THROUGH OLD CHEYENNE

Rolling out of the Old West, the Cheyenne Frontier Days parades recall a colorful era of the American scene. At 9:30 on the opening Saturday, and on Tuesday, Thursday and the final Saturday of every Frontier Week, the aerial rocket explodes and the Old West passes in review.

In 1927, the Frontier Committee selected the "Evolution of Transportation" as its parade theme. That marked the beginning of the parades as we know them today. Bursting with historical significance, the four parades showcase a world-class collection of horse-drawn vehicles... historical floats... marching bands... equestrian units... antique automobiles... drill teams... clowns... and so much more.

Through the years, the Frontier Days parades have evolved into a colorful pageant of the Frontier West, mixing the nostalgia of yesteryear with the excitement of today.

Participation, whether on horseback, in a marching band, dressed in old-fashioned duds and seated in a carriage, or watching curbside, "going to the parade" is part of Frontier Week for Cheyenne's citizens and visitors alike. Our photo albums are filled with snapshots that record these processions of charming splendor.

The Tivoli Building was the site of the first meeting to organize a Frontier Day in August 1897.

Jim Murphy and his beautiful horses pleased the crowds at both the night shows and the parades, 1960.

Banners and flags fluttered while vendors sold all manner of things from tents as the military marched through the parade in 1923.

🥾 Jim Nelson drove a covered wagon with Prairie Rose Henderson at his side, 1927.

🥾 Harry Shapiro drove the family buggy wearing the proper outfit. He is a Cheyenne native and still lives in the house where he was born. The photograph was taken about 1930.

🥾 The Thompson twins, Bill and Bob, rode with Mrs. Mark Chapman, July 21, 1929.

ALL DRESSED UP!

Ladies in old-time regalia strike a sassy pose. They are Mrs. W.J. Robitaile, Mrs. Elizabeth Fisher, Mrs. R.T. Coyle, Mrs. Margaret Artist.

Helen Bowen loved to ride in the parades. She won many rodeo honors between 1912 and 1915.

The Thompson twins, Bill and Bob, rode a tandem in the mid-1930s. They are the sons of Tribune editor, John Charles Thompson.

In 1960, the Lummis children wore clothing from the family's attic. They are Doran (Del), age five; Cynthia, seven, Claudia, eight, and Christine, nine

Winners of a kids' costume contest pose for the Tribune photographer, Francis Brammer, c. 1939.

YOUNG RIDERS

Chief Iron Shells (Norman Knox) stands with Jerry and Patti Reed.

1945 cowgirl Janane Bolt is ready to ride.

Nancy and Sally Black are ready for the parade. Nancy grew up to be Miss Frontier in 1955.

Written on the back: "Jarg Johnson's daughter and son on Bullet." Bullet was King Merritt's famous horse, the daughter, Judy, and the son, Jim; he grew up to be the current CFD parade chairman.

48

For a parade in 1957, the Women in the Air Force (WAF) band set the pace.

Iona Yvonne Setzer on Dakota Buck performed unusual tricks during a 15-minute program at the rodeo in 1943; they also appeared in the parades.

'40s AND '50s

An automobile advertised Victory Bonds during World War II.

The Saddle Tramps carried the flags of all 48 states, c. 1940.

A Wyoming Air National Guard model jet always stayed on the ground, c. 1950.

50

Indian dancers performed from a wagon, c. 1950.

Murial Mitchell and friends looked over an empty branding float at Frontier Park.

The Indian float was pulled by mules in 1940.

TRADITION PERSISTS:
INDIANS AND THE UNION PACIFIC

Indians and buffalo ride on the Union Pacific float under the words, "Development of the Glorious West."

This Union Pacific float, with a survey crew, gandy dancers and construction supervisors, no longer appears in the parades. Photograph c. 1936.

Jay Farris furnished horses and drove them in the 1960s.

All sorts of music enlivened the parades.

HAVING FUN

 Rodeo clown George Stewart, his mule Josephine, and Beverly Nair made a big hit with the mammoth overalls, c. 1955.

 Parade, 1947. The two-man band tootled through the parade.

 Flag Bearers: Flo Walterschied, Dorothy Portes and Yvonne Setzer Busing lead the Union Pacific section. Old-timers will remember the long-gone businesses in the background.

Barbie Wester, Jo Adsit Fowler, Jean Brown, Shirley Humphrey, Marlene Larson, Luce Anspaugh and Marge Lesser danced on the Red Dog Saloon Float, 1962.

THE DANCE HALLS

Earlier, Jane Devine, Katie Connaghan and Eve Souply rode on the "beer float," c. 1945.

Cara Baber, Carolyn Wheeler, and Barbara Moran relax after kicking up their heels on Dazee's Dance Hall Float in 1963.

Everyone had fun on "Hells Half Acre," the beer float!

Jean Nimmo Dubois was honored in 1981 for 50 years of faithful participation in Frontier Days.

The venerable old Tivoli stood guard over the parades in 1995.

🥾 Miss Frontier Louise Holmes and Lady-In-Waiting Bette McIvor accompanied visiting dignitaries on the stagecoach ride from the depot to the Plains Hotel, 1939.

EVERYONE LOVES A PARADE

🥾 The Frontier Committee took the mud wagon to Denver's St. Patrick's Day parade, 1993.

🥾 Two Bar Seven ranch trailed into town from south of Laramie for many years.

The Society For The Preservation And Encouragement Of Barbershop Quartet Singing In America makes melodious music and madcap fun along the way. Maurice Oestereich is in the tub.

Full of mirth and merriment, the Chugwater Philharmonic String Quartet entertains throughout the parade.

Mel Pennington rode Windy, 1940.

Oral E. Ross drove a covered wagon in 1965.

The early morning hitch-up is a time for coffee and conversation. Larry Romsa, team contractor, stands on the right.

60

 The shrine clowns "warm up" the crowd before the parade begins. Harold Russell smiles under his make-up, 1974.

BEGINNINGS

On matched sorrel horses, Sheriff Posse members Ralph Middleton, Joe Shaker, Dr. Jack Ketchum and Kenny Fogg display their flag along with Old Glory.

Miss Mary Hickey watched the onlookers, c. 1985.

AND ENDINGS

 The ride itself brought memories back to this elderly rider.

Dr. James Clark has impersonated pioneer preacher Dr. Marcus Whitman for twenty years. Mrs. Clark waves from the other side of the buggy.

62

Wyoming's own gracious Governor Nellie Tayloe Ross entertained visitors from Vice President Charles Dawes to Indian chiefs in 1925.

To Harry Hynds
my dear friend.
Best wishes
Wallace Beery,
Pony Express Co,
Luskytimans Players

P.S. I am not the one sitting on the horse—

WALLACE BERRY CHEYENNE FRONTIER DAYS 1925

PEOPLE

From the beginning, visitors have flocked here to be a part of the great celebration. George Eastman, of Kodak fame, was a spectator in 1897 and remarked, "If we only had a moving picture of that show!" Other visitors quickly caught "Kodak" fever and have snapped photos of the events and each other for a century.

In the days before radio and television, part of the entertainment was the music. Bands played on every street corner and all through the rodeo; they added the thump-thump of a march and the sweet strains of a melody to the proceedings. Actors of stage, screen, and radio came to Cheyenne to see and be seen. They mingled with the crowds, posed for innumerable photographs, and sometimes, in the mid-'20s, tried their hand at bronc riding or bull dogging. Glamorous female stars became part of the scene, too, in a less strenuous manner. Politicians stopped in Cheyenne for a handshake and a headline.

The hallmark of Cheyenne Frontier Days is tradition, and no tradition at the "Daddy of 'em All" is more meaningful than the participation of the Native Americans. They have played a key role in every Cheyenne Frontier Days celebration except the first. They have enthralled spectators with their gorgeous costumes, haunting music and colorful dances.

According to historian Milt Riske, actor Bill Hart was scheduled to be present for the 1925 show. He did not attend, but Wallace Beery came in his place. On the back of the photo, Beery is described as being in a "disruptable outfit driving a bull calf pulled wagon." The passenger is child actor, Vondelle Darr, and the man on the horse is Charles B. Irwin.

Douglas Fairbanks loved rodeo and often came to Frontier Days.

🤠 Mark McEwan, from the CBS Morning Show, joined the Chugwater Philharmonic for one strum of Carl Halladay's guitar.

🤠 Bob Mathews, fiddler with the Chugwater gang, and super model Cindy Crawford share a laugh.

MUSICIANS

🤠 Larry Peterson, sometime Philharmonic member and always professional radio announcer, interviewed a Thunderbird pilot.

🤠 "Chugwater Band, 1911-12 or 13 (Probably 1912)" is written on the back of this photograph.

Cheyenne's own Amy and Annie Smith entertained at a Pancake Breakfast.

Margaret Howe and friend stood close to Lawrence Welk, 1951.

They liked Myron Floren, too...

...and Rocky Rockwell.

Mickey Powers treasures this photograph with its personalized autographs of Guy Madison and Andy Devine, c. 1952.

Screen stars Bill Elliott and Vera Ralston flank Lady-In-Waiting Susan Murray and Miss Frontier Ann Dinneen, 1947.

Bob Nolan from the singing group Sons of the Pioneers made friends with local children in 1947.

CHEYENNE WELCOMES CELEBRITIES

The McIntires and Merritts were good friends and visited each other often.

Willie Nelson.

Left: Sally Rand rustled her feathers here in 1935. Inset: In 1994, Ross and Lois Moor (Lois Crain, Miss Frontier 1934) revisited the log home in Frontier Park where she was raised. Her father, Charlie, was caretaker at the park from the late 1920s until his death in 1949.

THE ENTERTAINERS

👢 Senator Francis Warren and movie star Tim MCoy conferred on a long-forgotten point, c. 1925. McCoy lived in Cheyenne 1919-1921 and served as Adjutant General of Wyoming before leaving to make his mark in Hollywood.

THE POLITICIANS

👢 Two gentlemen, Governor Milward Simpson and Arthur Godfrey, rode in the parades together, 1956.

👢 Governor Lester C. Hunt surveyed his domain from the Capitol steps, 1945.

Larry Birleffi, Curt Gowdy and Governor Ed Herschler paid close attention to the rodeo in 1975.

It was a grand day in July 1990, when President George Bush came to call.

Another shutterbug caught Joseph Shimitz photographing bronc rider Lois Phillips.

R.R. Doubleday posed with the glamorous cowgirls he so often photographed in the 1920s.

Doubleday pasted his image onto the action-filled bronc riding scene.

👢 For three years in the 1940s, Barney and Larry Grandpre helped their father, William, water down the track. One year they hooked a hayrack to a team of horses to pick up cans and bottles on the rodeo grounds.

👢 Bob St. Clair dressed the part to volunteer in the 1930s.

👢 John Cook first visited Cheyenne in 1927 when he was 16. That year, he patronized a photographer's booth for this souvenir. After moving to Cheyenne, he worked as a volunteer for 40 years and proudly wore a Heels badge.

PHOTOGRAPHERS AND MODELS

Bob Pearson posed with a pretty lady whose identity has been forgotten.

👢 Francis Brammer covered the CFD scene for many years. This 1956 promotional photo is typical.

👢 Visitors to Cheyenne Frontier Days in 1906 could have their photographs made into post cards for souvenirs of the great event.

All the Indians brought their best costumes to Frontier Days. The chief is saying, "Let's dance!"

Committeemen's children, Bill Brewster, Mickey Powers and John Brewster made friends with the Indians.

THE INDIANS

From a note written by Charles Aylward: "The Indian village held a great mystique for Beverly Aylward when she was a child."

Inscribed on the back of the photo on the left is, "Quite a cute little Indian girl. She danced nicely while her father played the tom-tom." Mary Richardson, center, and her husband (Willie) stand with an unidentified guest. On the back of the photo on the right Mrs. Richardson wrote, "He likes being photographed and most of all he likes the accompanying coins.".

Miss Frontier 1977, Nancy Borthwick, and an Indian child smile for the camera.

Indian children were friends of Jeanette Tyrrell, Miss Frontier 1956, and her Lady-In-Waiting Lynn Mabee.

Miss Frontier Helen McCarty and her Lady-In-Waiting Louise Holmes stand amid a forest of feathers, 1938.

 Young cowboys, Norman and Wayne Neeman, are dwarfed by the large tipi.

 Hoop Dancers are crowd pleasers.

Indian kids preen before a parade, 1984.

A proud Sioux carefully applied make-up and dressed in his traditional garments in 1977.

78

👢 Dust jacket from a 78-rpm record. Hank Thompson and the Brazos Valley Boys played for dancing in the old Pavilion, c. 1953.

PARTIES, PLACES AND PLAYTIME

Frontier Week resembles a crazy quilt. There are happenings of every size and description. Although the rodeo serves as the background fabric to hold the whole thing together, each pattern piece is an entity unto itself. Some are made of glossy satin, others of colorful gingham or sturdy denim.

The Coronation Ball kicks off the events, followed by the Cheyenne Frontier Days Invitational Art Show and Sale. Both are held before the RODEO begins on the first Saturday.

Cheyenneites fling out the welcome mat for visitors and for each other. Party-goers, quivering with energy and excitement, patronize the dance halls downtown, go to the carnival on Frontier Park grounds, and tap their toes to the beat of Country/Western music during the Night Show. Having fun during Frontier Week has always been serious business.

Getting cowboys and kids together has always been something special, too. Get cowboys and special kids together and you have something exceptional---Exceptional Rodeo. This denim and straw hat event has captured the hearts of all who participated, from Frontier Days royalty to clowns and champion cowboys.

The rodeo has been held on the same site, Frontier Park, since 1908. The facilities have changed through the years. The Indian Village has been relocated several times, fencing moved and removed, and old buildings have been torn down while others have been built. Aerial photographs have recorded these changes.

Jennifer DeKock came from DeMott, Indiana, to enjoy the rodeo in 1995. Contestant 14 is listed as Gip Allen.

Six friends, Pete Peterson, Nathal "Occ" Occhipinti, Otis Kitchen, Bob St. Clair and Dexter Brown, liberated the huge overalls from a Western store about 1950. The woman is not identified except as "Pete Peterson's girl friend."

Everyone loved to dance at the Mayflower.

J. T. Wilkinson, Ramona Merritt, Dale Harris, Cotton Merritt, Ginger Merritt Harris, Dede Hayes Merritt and Hyde Merritt enjoyed the PlayMor Club.

AFTER THE RODEO

During a party at the mayor's house, Australian Ambassador to the United States Larry Strange played the accordion, Clark Smith the wash tub bass and Wm. K. "Bill" Anderson the waste basket drum while the hostess, Joan Nation, overlooked the fun.

Horse racing was a big part of Frontier Days for nearly 85 years. In a 1949 photo finish, the winner was Chico Pearl.

300 yards for 2-year-olds and 3-year-olds, 1947. Winner, Frog W; owner, Milo Whitcomb, and rider, Bob Yeager.

Dean Merritt stood by his horse, Baldy Boy, the winner of a race in 1953.

AND THEY'RE OFF

The starting gate was pulled in front of C Stand where the race fans sat, c. 1960.

Off they go! Since 1954 the Thunderbirds have thrilled the public with their breathtaking formations.

IN THE SKY...
THE THUNDERBIRDS

The Thunderbird pilots and the Frontier Committee gathered for a photograph in 1981.

The 1995 cattle drive brought steers to Frontier Park for the timed events.

ON THE CATTLE DRIVE

Don Kensinger, right foreground, trail boss, directed the cattle drive in 1985. Some committeemen were good hands, others kept their hands on the saddle horn.

Too much to look at!

The Midway, 1994.

AT THE CARNIVAL

Ferris wheels spin in the sunset.

87

Kiwanis Club members flip pancakes for 10,000 hungry guests each Monday, Wednesday and Friday at the Indian Committee function.

DOWNTOWN

The Gunslingers prepare to "hang" a bad 'un, 1995.

Little Tracy Wiejek watches her mother, Jan, apply make-up for a rousing performance of the Melodrama.

Clown Rick Chatman helped with the activities at the Exceptional Rodeo in 1993.

Lots of action and smiles accompany the ridin' and ropin'. Everyone wins a prize.

EXCEPTIONAL RODEO

Grounds Chairman Kurt Peth cheered on a bronc buster in 1995.

 Melanie Knight and her cowboy enjoyed being a part of the rodeo for special kids.

Cheyenne photographer Joseph Shimitz had this picture made into a post card.

Charles B. Irwin, seated, drove his buffalo team for the amusement of Col. Theodore Roosevelt during Frontier Days, 1910. Sam Brownell, rancher north of Cheyenne, stands with his back to camera. The third man is unidentified.

The Denver team beat the Cheyenne Indians, 11-0.

HAVING FUN

Trick roping and other specialty acts headlined the night shows before the glittering Nashville stars appeared in the 1970s.

Mounted cavalry units dashed through death-defying drills until the Army was motorized prior to World War II.

The costume contest showcases fashions from bygone days. Haydee and Johanna Dijkstral model beautiful hand-made garments.

Gaye Harrell displayed an 1860s ball gown made by Jimmie Thornton.

OLD WEST

The models pose on the west steps of the Capitol Building.

Holly Beumee created her afternoon dress in the style of 1890.

The always popular Laybourn family wears clothes made by Felicity Laybourn Lynch.

Glenna Hirsig sported a long, divided skirt. Bob Schrader escorted the contestants down the stairs.

ON PARADE

Jennifer Georges showed an 1890s style wedding dress made by Holly Beumee.

Bob Schrader wore the outfit used by his grandfather, Wesley Schrader, in the mortuary business.

Miss Frontier Kathleen Keefe, Governor Cliff Hansen, Lady-In-Waiting Carolyn Holmes and Mayor Herb Kingham lead the dancing in 1966.

Bill Linderman, Miss Frontier Margy Hirsig, Casey Tibbs, Lady-In-Waiting Nancy Black and Jim Shoulders, 1954.

CORONATION BALL

Jack Crews presented his daughter, Libby, at her coronation as Miss Frontier in 1985.

1931 Miss Frontier Jean Nimmo Dubois was escorted into the Coronation Ball, 1995, amid pomp & circumstance.

Governor Jim and Sherri Geringer visited with artist Roy Kerswill as Ruth Storey, sales clerk, looked on.

Artists and patrons crowded into the Old West Museum for the stellar show and sale, 1994.

Artists and special guests relished a party at the Shellback Ranch the evening before the grand opening, 1995.

THE ART SHOW

👢 The Lane Frost statue dedication, 1994, attracted a large crowd. Lane Frost died in 1989 from injuries sustained in a rodeo accident.

👢 The artists lined up for their annual group picture, 1995.

98

Photographer J.E. Stimson provided a record of the first Frontier Day, 1897.

Changes at Frontier Park can be studied through aerial photographs like this one from 1929.

👢 The campgrounds were north of 8th Avenue and east of Carey, where Lions Park is today.

PARK EVOLUTION

👢 A rustic gate stood guard at the Frontier Village on the night show grounds, c. 1929.

👢 Tourist homes did a brisk business for many years. This photograph was taken in 1937.

100

 The ticket office on the right was west of B Stand, and the tent in the upper left housed a night show act, c. 1954.

In 1966, Bill Nation took an aerial photograph of Frontier Park.

General Chairman Dick Sherman, Gary Carver, Harry Speltz, Howard Wiggert, Ken Tobin and Wally Reiman start construction of the East Stand, 1991.

The Vandewark Wing of the Old West Museum opened in June 1992.

Greg and Monica Wahl rode their unicycles through town to promote the rodeo, 1959.

A nameless volunteer feeds breakfast to the longhorn steers.

THE VOLUNTEERS

For a century, the volunteer has been the fuel that stokes the engine of the world's greatest outdoor celebration. From the General Chairman to the rookie car parker, every Frontier Days volunteer has a vital role to play. Without each contribution, this annual get-together at the end of the high plains would be "just another local celebration" instead of the world renowned "Mardi Gras in Rawhide."

The General Committee is composed of 12 volunteer professional and business people. They head up a group of more than 2,500 volunteers who organize, produce and promote a celebration that revives, for one short period in July, the West as it was.

The backbone of the production at Frontier Days centers on the Heels, a men's volunteer service organization. Heels was founded during the Depression to replace paid arena help with volunteers. It was one way to save the show during those perilous times. The Heels have worked with the General Committee since 1935.

The diversity of tasks accomplished and years of service are astounding: gatekeepers may have guarded "their" spot for ten seasons; timers and judges of the rodeo events often claim twenty years, and parade marshals an equal number. Their only remuneration is knowing they did their part. Oh, yes, they did have some fun and camaraderie along the way.

As a salute for a job well done, since 1993 the General Committee has annually sponsored the Volunteer Appreciation Banquet to bring all the workers together. All 2,500, the whole gang, are the pride of Cheyenne Frontier Days; however, each committee nominates one member to receive a special award as Volunteer of the Year.

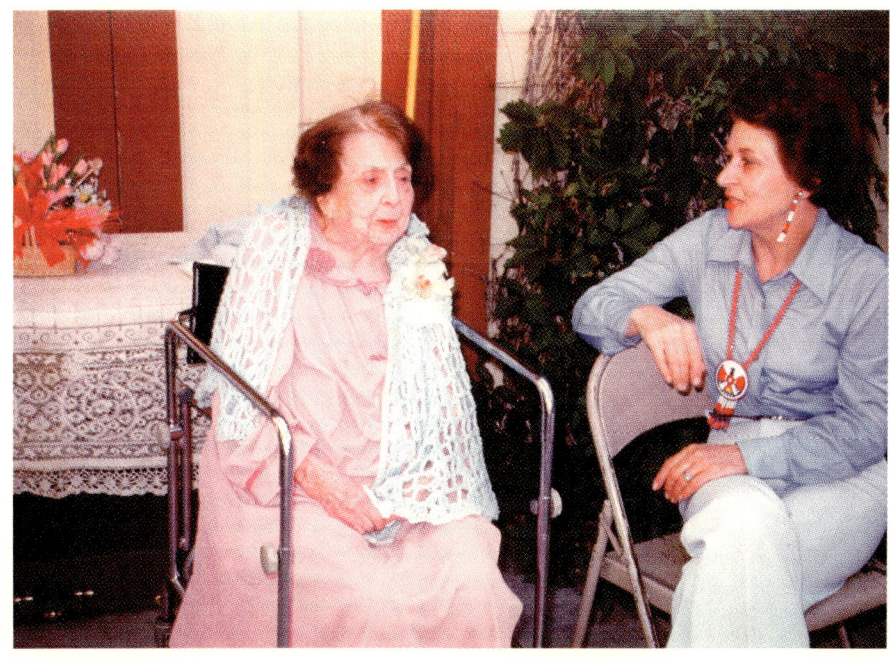

Dazee Bristol with
Thelma Brubaker, 1979.

ROYALTY

Lady-In-Waiting Norma Jean Bell and Miss Frontier Susan Murray, 1948, waved to the crowd.

Tammy Powers, 1989.

Rita Holmes and Trish Pattno stand with the Budweiser Team, 1981.

Miss Frontier Helen McCarty, Chairman Rudy Hofmann, and Lady-In-Waiting Louise Holmes made a winning team in 1938.

This formal portrait of Louise Holmes, Miss frontier 1939. was made into a post card.

Bob Mathews, fiddler for the Chugwater Philharmonic, watched Miss Frontier Rachelle Hayes toss out the first pitch at a Denver Zephers' game, 1993.

Miss Frontier Rachelle Hayes and her Lady-In-Waiting Tricia Weppner were able spokesmen for Frontier Days in 1993.

Dr. Jack Ryan, Ace Tyrrell, Jim Powers, John Bell and an unidentified partner ran Frontier Days, c. 1950.

Jim Powers and Otis Melton admired the mule named Jim P.

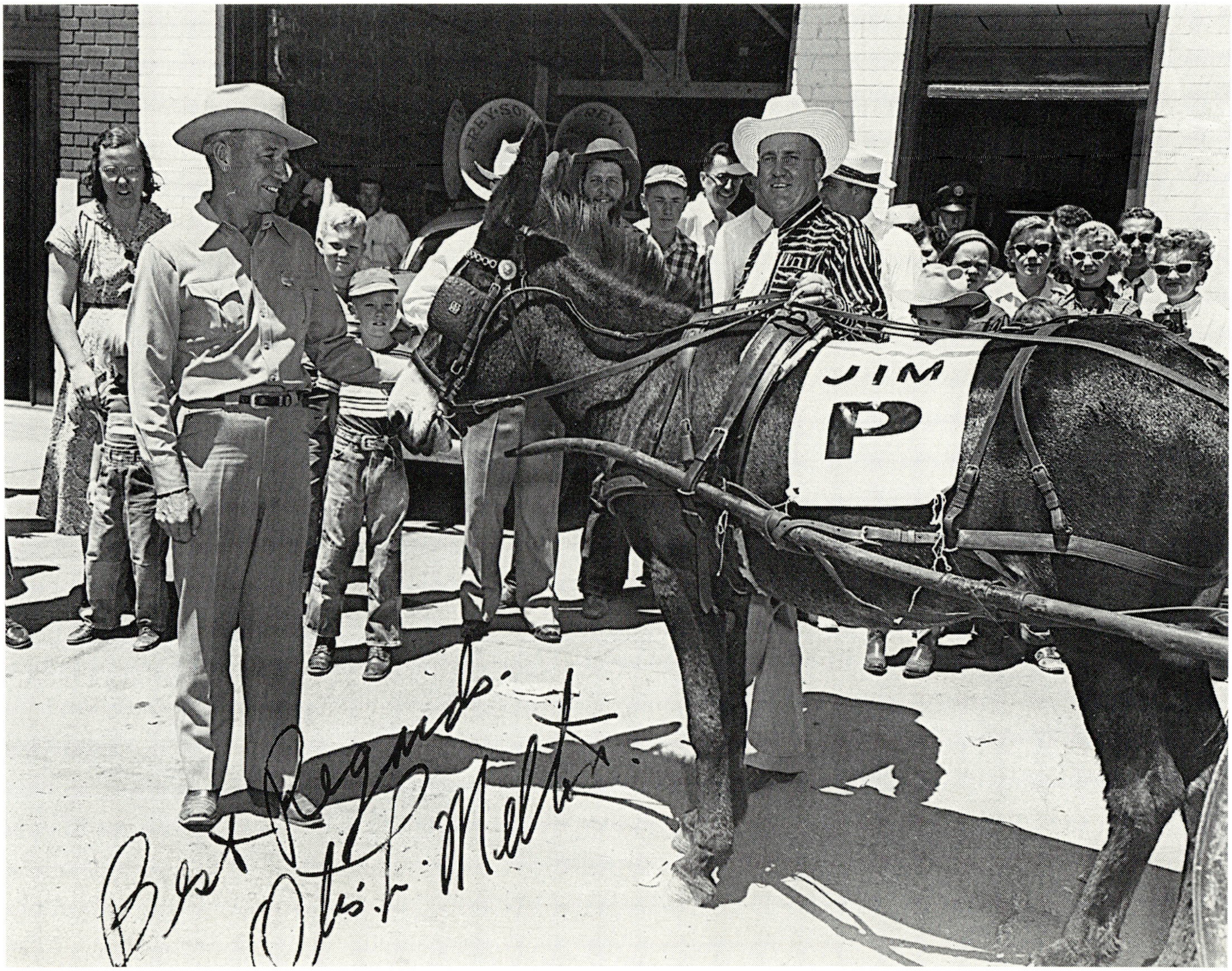

👢 To have some fun, the first committee took a Sunday drive with mixed-up equipment.

👢 Cowboys and committeemen relax in Chute 10 after the rodeo

COMMITTEEMEN

👢 The 1994 committee had fun as they posed for this photograph in old-fashioned gear.

110

🥾 The 1910 American Underslung was owned by C. W. Hirsig, standing on the left.

Shirley Holmes Churchill and Buddy Hirsig, arena director. Miss Frontier in 1979, today Shirley and her husband, Brad Churchill, are stock contractors and work with Harry Vold.

In 1995, Gus Fleischli was given a well-deserved award for his many years of service to CFD.

ARENA FOLK

Past chairman Kent Rutledge confers with stock contractor Harry Vold, 1993.

Chute Boss Don Kensinger presides over the rough stock events.

👢 Arlene Kensinger sits tall as director of the Dandies, 1995.

👢 The Dandies of Daddy of 'em All were organized in 1970. Each year, 16 teenage girls serve as ambassadors on horseback.

Sometimes the Dandies leave their horses at home and try a pickup for size, 1990.

DANDIES

Rachelle Hayes rode as a Dandy three years before becoming Miss Frontier. Arlene Kensinger became a close friend.

Lilo Jessup, a Dandy, modeled the parade costume for the Centennial of Wyoming Statehood celebration in 1990.

114

Four generations of Dinneens have volunteered for Frontier Days. Jim Dinneen is being shown the ropes by his father Bill Jr. and his grandfather Bill Sr., whose father "W.E." was on the second Frontier Committee in 1898.

Mike Brown wrote, "This haircut provided many photo opportunities for tourists and gave me free access to the rodeo."

FAMILY TRADITIONS

For a publicity picture, Buddy Hirsig helped his sister Margy, Miss Frontier, and Lady-In-Waiting Nancy Black brand a calf, 1954.

Steers and horses require regular care and must be in the proper places for events that run like clockwork.

◆ After hoisting the hay bales into place for a pancake breakfast, the Indian Committee volunteers rested on their laurels.

VOLUNTEERS AT WORK

◆ Volunteer photographer Jim Lynch records the winning chuckwagon team.

◆ One representative from each committee is selected to ride in the parade on Volunteer Day.

118

The Public Relations committee administers a public dousing to their retiring chairman. They caught Pete McNiff, (above) in 1981...and Tim LaHiff (right) in 1995.

🌶 Retirement parties are held all over the park after the finals. A properly set table, pithy signs and the Bartles and James "boys" add to the fun.

FOND FAREWELL

Ned Murray, left, presented Chairman Lou Domenico with "Lil Lou," a restored popcorn wagon, in 1965. Domenico gave the historic vehicle to the Frontier Days Carriage Collection, and it can now be seen in the Old West Museum.

Bill Obermeier drove a Yellowstone coach filled with costumed women in 1951. The riders included Mesdames R. J. Boesel; Peter Appel, Jr.; Gus Fleischli, Jr., holding Kirk; William McInerney; L. C. Russell; Walter Appel; Judy Brucher; E. A. Groves; William Quinn and R. A Templin.

Bob Walston, veteran parade driver, handled a team of mules, c. 1960.

I LOVE A PARADE

Carrol Orrison, local Budweiser distributor, introduced a Clydesdale to a young friend in 1979.

Model Cindy Crawford rewarded Indian Committee members Gene Engrav and Pete Wiejek with a hug.

A Booster Trip took Lady-In-Waiting Margy Hirsig and Miss Frontier Carole Rees to Las Vegas in 1953. They waved their greetings to friends at home.

ON THE MOVE

 Photographer Francis Brammer caught the flavor of Western hospitality in 1954 with Miss Frontier Margy Hirsig and Lady-In-Waiting Nancy Black.

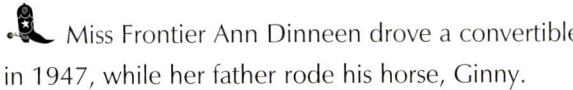 Miss Frontier Ann Dinneen drove a convertible in 1947, while her father rode his horse, Ginny.

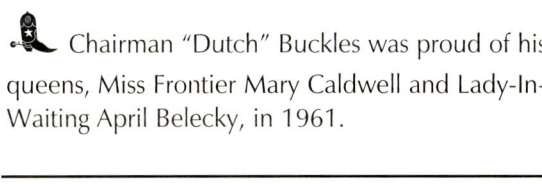 Chairman "Dutch" Buckles was proud of his queens, Miss Frontier Mary Caldwell and Lady-In-Waiting April Belecky, in 1961.

Mary Liz Carpender was named Person of the Year by the Cheyenne Chamber of Commerce in 1981 in recognition of her volunteer work on the parades. Her husband, Julian, stands on the left, and Chamber President Tom Kilty on the right.

Dorothy Richardson has ridden side saddle in the Union Pacific section of the parades since 1948.

 For the 100th Annual celebration, over three hundred people submitted recipes, then baked and tasted them, to create the elegant Cheyenne Frontier Days™ cookbook. This representative group sampled old-style coffee on the prairie.

"W.E." Dinneen was a member of the second Frontier Days committee in 1898; family members have volunteered every year since.

Frank Tate worked as groundskeeper at Frontier Park in the 1950s.

Edythe Baird operated the switchboard for many years.

In 1952 chuckwagon racing was introduced to Frontier Days. This panel judged the event. The men in the top row are unidentified. Middle row: unidentified, Dr. Jack Ryan, Chairman Jim Powers, unidentified and Roy Volk. Seated: Fred Porter, Sr., Fred Porter, Jr., Hap Hanes, and the next two are unidentified.

On four Saturdays in early summer, hundreds of volunteers report for work at 8:00 a.m.

This crew moved file cabinets and set up desks. Duane Roedocker, the man on the left, (above), supervised the work.

 A brigade of gardeners set out to do battle with the tall grass and weeds.

WORK DAY

 Other crews installed siding or moved lumber or did landscaping.

130

BUILDING THE IMAGE

To build an image, Terry Bridwell, Tim LaHiff, Scott Binning and Kevin Keller posed for the camera.

THE WAGON DOCTORS

To maintain and preserve the 130-unit carriage collection, the Wagon Doctors work throughout the year. Upper left, Sam Amberson cuts wood; on the right Wes Coulson plies the wheelwright's skills; and lower left, Patty Johnston Austin polishes a brass lamp. Below, Tom Williams and Sam Amberson stand in front of a wagon being restored.

Phil Van Horn and Jerry Jessen work through many issues in guiding Frontier Days into its second century.

BOARD OF DIRECTORS

The Board of Directors for 1996. Standing: Dick Loseke, Terry Bridwell, Jim Gusea, Phil Van Horn, Dick Sherman, Ron Long and Gary Carver. Seated: Dave Pope, Bill Beaman, Chairman Jerry Jessen, Ken McCann and Tom Johnson.

👢 The Heels numbered about a dozen when they organized in 1936; by 1995, more than 300 were needed to do the work. This photograph was taken in 1993.

👢 Dick Patterson has been a Heel since 1976.

THE HEELS

The Heels sported very bright plaid shirts in 1937. Ed Storey and Charles Hirsig are on either end; Hirsig did not buy a shirt.

This clipping is from a scrapbook belonging to Ann Dinneen Smith. Her mother is seated on the right in the photograph.

 The name W-Heels was taken in 1941. At the time of this photo, in 1963, the group had grown to 22 members. Left, standing: Ann King, Katherine Halverson, Margurite Martin, Patricia Taylor, Margaret Cook, Mary Rohowitz, Maxine Keefe, Dazee Bristol, Elinor Robinson, Jackie Boice, Mary Helen Ausman, Patricia Baggs. Seated: Minnie Holbrook, Ruth Benton, Mary Liz Carpender, Margaret Boice, Grace Porter, Mary Carpenter. Floor: Cay Ziemer, Linda McInerney, Louise Pennoyer, Armella Benton.

The note on the back reads, "Four W-Heels admiring hats, shoes and dresses donated to the costume collection." The Hansom cab in the background is being "doctored." From the left; Elinor Robinson, Louise Cole, Beverly Vandehei and Katherine Halverson, 1978.

THE W-HEELS

Parade Marshals Mary Carpenter and Minnie Holbrook rode on pinto ponies named Salt and Pepper, 1952.

W-Heels, 1993. Back row: Mary Weppner, Patsy Pattno, Tuda Crews, Jane Uchner, Susan Lewis, Louise Bartlett, Diane Humphrey, Pat Kennedy, Glenna Hirsig, Norma Morris, Peggy Hearne, Chris Ferguson. Middle row: Nancy Rutledge, Helen Pickett, Vanda Carroll, Sally Allen, Carol Farthing, Shirley Flynn, Ann Dinneen, Louise Cole. Front row: Dede Picket, Marietta Dinneen, Enid Lummis, Nancy Lawler, Karen Vencill, and Eileen Dinneen.

The Dandies line up for a presentation. Arlene Kensinger and Diane Humphrey, directors, are in front.

EVERYBODY

Miss Frontier Lois Crain opened the festivities in 1934. She was the first Miss Frontier chosen by the committee. From 1931 to 1933, they were chosen by a community-wide vote.

SMILE!

To revive a tradition, a panorama was taken in 1986.

🤠 "Last Day of Ol' J", 1992. Demolition on the old, East side grandstand was started immediately after the Sunday Finals, 1992.

First Day of the new East stand, 1993. volunteers line up in fornt of "Ol J's" replacement on opening day.

RINGING IN

The 100th Annual Committee. Standing: Kay Jessen, Scott Binning, Terry Bridwell, Jeanne Bryan, Mike Lane, Bill Dubois, Dick Sherman, Marietta Dinneen, Dave McCracken, Floyd Humphrey. Seated: Jack Ferguson, Pete Goodrich, Tim LaHiff, Bill Beaman and Jim Gusea pictured at the New Year's Eve celebration.

THE 100TH YEAR

The General committee. From the left: Scott Binning, Larry Shippy, Roger Schreiner, Gary Child, Jim Johnson, Chairman Phil Van Horn, Grant Fleming, Bob Haberkorn, Bob Ortega, Dean Schroeder and Col. Tucker Fagan.

100th ANNIVERSARY YEAR VOLUNTEER BANQUET

Volunteers of the Year: Back row; Steve Berg, Contract Acts; Dan Wanea, Indians; Jeff Rayment, Concessions; Corey Fulzone, Grounds; John Kuster, Parades; Roger Lawrence, Public Relations. Front row: Stovepipe Pette, Contestants; Tammy Shultz, Tickets; Barb Lutz, Military, and Mike Sandidge, Security.

👢 Governor Jim Geringer presented the Volunteer of the Year award to Mike Sandidge for his work on the Security committee.

👢 Five hundred members of the Frontier Days family met for dinner, the awards and dancing.

👢 Leonard Meyer, a volunteer for nearly 50 years, gave the invocation.

144

The Cheyenne Daily Sun-Leader.

VOL. XXX. --NO 281 CHEYENNE. WYOMING FRIDAY EVENING: AUGUST, 27, 1897. PRICE FIVE CENTS

BOYS' SCHOOL SUITS

SHORT OR LONG PANTS.

We have got anything you want in Boys' Clothing. We have always had a big stock of these goods, but its MUCH LARGER NOW THAN EVER. Cheap suits, or fine suits, and the prices we will guarantee as cheap as Chicago, Omaha or Denver. We have Boys' Knee Pants and Long Pants separate from suits.

M. MARKS.

One Week More Before FALL GOODS ARRIVE

Everything in the Line of Summer Goods Must be ClosedOut

Ladies' Knit Vests, former price 14c, now 8c.

Ladies' Knit Vests, former price 20c, now 12.c.

Ladies' Fine Ribbed Vests, former value 45c, now 27c. with or without sleeves.

Children's Ribbed Underwear at 23c each.

Gents' Fine Balbriggan Underwear, value 65c, at 49c each—chocolate, tan, green and blue.

Summer Corsets below cost to close out.

Princess Summer Corset, value 65c, at 35c pair.

Nonpareil Summer Corset, value $1, at 60c pair.

Ladies' Shirt Waists, former value $1, at 49c each.

Ladies' Shirt Waists ,former value $1.25, $1.35 and $1.50, at 75c each.

Outing Flannel 6c, 8c and 10c a yard.

36-inch Bleached Muslin, 6 1-2c yard

Best quality Check Gingham, 6c yd

Light Calico for Waists at 5c yard

Entire line of Ladies' and Misses' Oxfords and Slippers at COST.

Ladies' Kid-Oxfords ,value $1.25 and $1.35, 95c pair.

Ladies' Fine Kid Oxfords, value $1.50, and $1.75, at $1.20 pair.

Misses Kid Oxfords, value $1.50, at 95c pair.

Gents' Black Twilled Overshirts, value 65c, 44c each.

Gents' Black Sateen Shirts (fine quality), worth $1.50, at 95c each.

Balance of our Summer Dress Goods at less than cost.

P. S.—Agent for Triple Knee "Leather" Stockings. Full line just arrived, for boys and girls. At 25c pair.

WM. MYERS.

That's what everybody thinks who has tried our SODA and is qualified to speak about it. You can't be cool unless you pass the summer on a soda basis. Something cool inside means coolness all over. Drink however much you will, our soda will never hurt you. It's always and only refreshing, invigorating and beneficial, never injurious. Drink soda abolish thirst. Our soda will do it. It's the jolliest way imaginable to strike a cold wave. It's funny, but it's so. There's nothing in Cheyenne quite so cool as our soda, except those who drink it.

Palace Pharmacy Drug Co.

A. R. Troxell, Ph. G. Manager

Graduate St. Louis College of Pharmacy.

WHEAT OVER ONE DOLLAR

SEPTEMBER WHEAT SOLD ABOVE THE ONE HUNDRED CENT MARK IN CHICAGO.

At One Dollar Three and a Half Cents the Bull Clique Refused to Let Go Their Holdings—Corn and Provisions Were Also Affected by Wheat Excitement.

Chicago, Aug. 26.— ... first time since the pr... paign in wheat start... September wheat sold ... lar mark in Chicago. ... ter the opening $1.03 ... an advance over yes... price of 6 3-4c.

Even at that temptin... clique refused to let g... ings. Enough wheat c... ket to break the price ... time the closing bell s... brokers who are engi... stoutly denied that it ... There was, perhaps, a ... ciousness in the way th... to bid up. It was cu... on Monday, when p... sharply, that the poo... put up $400,000 in mar... tainly had their reve... rise was plainly due ... which is now swelle... include Joseph Lei... French, Allen Grier & ... Kenne of Wall street. ... er--George R. French ... distinctly above the su... secret that he has a ... bushels of September ... not much more than ... of contract wheat i... hardly anything com... immense short line of ... for export. This is th... now plays into the ha... combine.

The sudden rise of ... not reflected in any ot... in the country, with ... Minneapolis, where Se... from 92c to $1. St. ... 2c at one time, but rel... prices for December. ... ties were not given ... one item of foreign ne... influence. The fore... shortage is estimated ... total of 1,000,000,000 bu... expected to increase ... American wheat. Its ... pecially felt in Decemb...

is not supposed to be under the thumb of any clique.

Corn and provisions were both affected by the excitement in wheat. In corn the trading was enormous, and although an advance of but 1 1-8a1 1-4c was recorded, the feeling was very strong at the close. Closing prices for provisions were from 15 to 20 cents higher than yesterday.

DENVER POST-SCRIPTS.

A masked robber entered the Corner saloon at Rawlins, presented a big six-...

...country. This would very largely ... crease the Klondike exodus and suicide roster.

Chicago's prize bigamist married women in five different states, and was prospecting in the sixth when the strong hand of the law hit him a jolt between the shoulder blades.

A boy of 12 years named Przymuszyufki was arrested in St. Louis in a beastly state of intoxication. At least that was the pronunciation he gave his name as near as the painfully shocked police officers could catch it.

President McKinley visited the grave of old John Brown up in the Adirondacks and stood for a few moments with bowed head wondering if the soul of the old martyr was yet on its long distance march.

Subscribe for the Daily Sun-Leader, 50 cents per month.

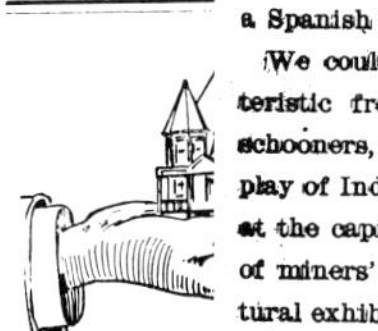

You can easily own ... want to. We have six ... which must be sold, ... a home for about one-t... to build the house, ... about the lots. For ... sell you a comparative ... house, full corner lot, ... per month, for $500. ... equally good. Call a... they are all gone.

Riner & ...

A FRIGHTFUL CUT

S. Bon's Sons Cut the ... mer Footwear Al...

All former cuts in s... ing compared with th...

Former prices cut ... must be sold and for ...

Child's Tan Vici, bu... 4 to 6, that were $1.35 ...

Child's Tan Vici, bu... 6 to 8, that were $1.5...

Misses Tan, button, ... to 2, that were $2.00, cut to $1.40.

Youths Tan, lace, 11 1-2 to 2, that were $2, cut to $1.10.

Ladies' Tan Oxfords, razor, coin and square toes, all sizes, 2 1-2 to 7, C, D, E, $1.75 grade, cut to $1.10.

Ladies' finest Tan Vici, $3 grade, Oxfords, only small sizes, 2 to 4, B and C widths, your choice for $1.00.

Ladies' Cloth and Linen Oxfords, 2 to 6, for $1.

Men's Tan Oxfords, comfort shoes, that were $3, cut to $1.75.

Men's Chocolate Russia Calf and Vici Shoes, $5 grade, cut to $3.60 and $2.75.

We have bunched all our men's tan shoes, $3 and $3.50 grades, cut to $1.95.

We have many other bargains too numerous to mention here.

We intend to make a big hole in our summer stock at these prices for the next ten days.

S. BON'S SONS

Daily Sun-Leader.

E. A. SLACK, PUBLISHER.

Entered at the Cheyenne, Wyo., Postoffice as Second Class Matter.

SUBSCRIPTION RATES.

Daily Sun-Leader, 1 year........ 6.00

Daily Sun-Leader, a month..... .50

Weekly Sun-Leader, 1 yr in adv. $2.00

FRIDAY, AUGUST 27, 1897.

FRONTIER DAY.

Why should not Cheyenne have a day of celebration the same as other towns? And what is the matter with us that we can't get up a hot time and call in all our neighbors? Inasmuch as this is one of the oldest towns in the far west, it is suggested that we choose for a title, "Frontier Day." A very good name, indeed, for a place that for so many years was an outfitting point for the north and west, and from which Indian supplies were freighted in wagons, and where subsequently the gay and festive cowboy rode through our streets as proudly as a Spanish hidalgo.

We could readily provide a characteristic frontier exhibition of prairie schooners, mounted cowboys and a display of Indian relics might be collected at the capital as well as a fine display of miners' products. Also an agricultural exhibit could be shown our neighbors that would open their eyes. Then there could be a little excursion on the side to the Hereford ranch, which is worth going miles to see.

All of the railroads will gladly cooperate in the project ,giving very low rates and helping to advertise the occasion. The Union Pacific will make a $2 round trip rate from Denver and Mr. Angier tells us he will secure very favorable rates from points east and west of Cheyenne. Superintendent Rasback says he will secure a cheap rate from Orin Junction for the round trip, and Agent Holliday says: ',Count the Burlington in on the celebration. We will gladly co-operate in doing honor to 'Frontier Day.'"

The Cheyenne club has not yet fixed the day of its bicycle tournament at the fair grounds, and we see no reason why it should not accept Frontier Day. Arrangements can also be made for a match game of baseball on the same grounds, to which the Union Pacific would run special trains at a rate of 15 cents for the round trip. The expense, which is the usual bugbear, would be very small. Mr. Angier says that they need not exceed $150 for music and everything. Surely this modest sum could be raised by subscription. A few years ago Mr. Angier brought 600 people up from Denver on a regular train, much to the surprise of all concerned in the affair, and without any special inducements being offered by our citizens. He is satisfied we can make a growing success of "Frontier Day" in Cheyenne if we only make the start. Each year will increase the interest outside in the event and make it easier to secure a large attendance.

We suggest that a meeting of our citizens be called at an early date and the program arranged so that the announcement may go forth unto the people. At this meeting full information as to railroad rates will be furnished and a day for the first celebration can be agreed upon. Let our business men take hold of the enterprise with their old time vim and it will certainly succeed.

The columns of the Sun-Leader are open for suggestions, but too much time must not be wasted in deliberation. In selecting a day we should bear in mind that Denver celebrates its Mountain and Plain Festival on Oct. 3 ,4 and 5. It has been proposed that Cheyenne choose Sept. 23.

...port and rise through the car just as it was getting speedy. He coolly walked after her, and just before the fatal leap grasped her firmly to his manly bosom. She struggled, but he only tightened his grip, saying: "Madam, you shan't throw off ... yourself!" When she got her breath she shrieked, "You big fool, I was only going out on the platform to wave my handkerchief to my friends." A party of Bangor yachtsmen aboard the train applauded the drummer for his heroism fully half an hour at intervals thereafter.—Springfield Republican.

Go to The Fair Store for Slates Pencils, Tablets, fine stationery and all other scho olsupplies. Prices the lowest.

GRAND ARMY SELECTIONS

J. P. S. GOBIN FOR COMMANDER IN CHIEF AND CINCINNATI FOR NEXT ENCAMPMENT.

Four Candidates Were Placed in Nomination and on the Second Ballot Gobin Was Elected—San Francisco Was Cincinnati's Rival, but the Former City Withdrew.

Buffalo, Aug. 26.—Cincinnati's triumph in securing the national encampment for 1898 and Pennsylvania's ...tory in winning the commader in ...hief of the Grand Army were the features of the encampment. Both battles ...ere hard fought. The struggle was ...ecipitated immediately after the executive session was called to order. ...he selection of the next place of meeting was first taken up, and the rival ...ties were given a hearing.

The city committee of Cincinnati ...as admitted and M. E. Ingalls, president of the Big Four railroad, present... the claims and attractions of the ...ty in a happy speech.

Delegate Woodruff of California pre...nted the claims of San Francisco.

On the first ballot Cincinnati received ... votes and San Francisco 214. The ...te had not been announced when Mr. ...oodruff withdrew San Francisco and ...ked that the selection of Cincinnati ... made unanimous. This was agreed by acclamation.

MRS. ANGELL'S CASE STILL ON.

Has Not Collapsed, Say the New York Attorneys of the Gould Estate.

New York, Aug. 26.—The case of Mrs. Sarah Ann Angell against the heirs of Jay Gould for dower rights has not collapsed. Although ex-Judge Dillon, attorney for the Goulds, obtained evidence from the mother and sister of Mrs. Angell to show that Mrs. Angell's claim was groundless, the suit will go go on, said one of Gould's attorneys, until it is dismissed by the plaintiffs or is tried by jury. Conspiracy to extort money is charged by the attorneys for the Goulds, and they say that Mrs. Angell is merely a tool. A designing woman is at the bottom of the whole affair, they say, and this is the woman who has been supplying money to Mrs. Cody of Denver with which to pay the lawyers and the expenses of the suit. The whole affair, they say, is nothing more than a bold scheme to extort money from the Goulds, and the supposition is that the plot was to play upon the sensibilities of the female members of the family by etxensive publicity and secure money without the necessity of a trial. David D. Duncan said today:

"We know the woman, but we are not yet prepared to make any statement concerning her. It will be revealed all in due time."

Ex-Judge Dillon said the same thing

BOOM AT HARTVILLE.

...t Work Hauling

...at visitors from ...ted camp must ... scene at this ...hat the railroad ... and determined ... much ore as is ...tting on extra .... The long line ... teams hauling ...ore are suggest... Wyoming when ...r miles in wag...id to present a ...earance at this ... day in the last ...ader has chron...heyenne of vari...h six and eight ... heavy wagons ...ey had been en...n the Good For...

...in the city from ...n who, with six ...s, a large Bain ...agon pulled by ...s bound for the ... has been found ... in hauling the ... been but a short ... of horses and ... shipped to the ... while recently ...nd wagons were ...force from Raw...

... camp which is ...me to the north...ounty as a God... the entire state ...ated though felt ... day as the com...rations.

... THE PEN.

...her who is dem...ple that small ...on the Laramie ...he penitentiary ...n. With wheat ... can be raised at ...oming soil, and ...ortly when the ...nd Little Lara... their attention ... grain. It could ...-product to the ... desire, and in ... increasing the ... ranches.

...Unrah, national ...en's Christian ...n the city, the ...n. Mrs. Unrah ... the rescue and ...ization and ar... made for her ... the Methodist ... the subject of ...e she will tell ...e and some of ...f crime in con...y work of the ...ill be clear and plain, but clothed in such delicate language that no one will take offense. Mrs. Nurah is said to be one of the best speakers of the day, and her experience in this line enables her not only to interest but instruct. Everybody invited. Admission, free. A collection will be taken for the work.

PILLOWS AND PINCUSHIONS.

The young ladies of the Sunergie of St. Mark's will offer for sale at 1710 Ferguson street, on Saturday afternoon and evening, Aug. 28, the very latest in sofa pillows and pincushions, silk embroidered, including wheel club colors. Cake or sandwiches and coffee, 15c.

ITALIAN SWORDSMANSHIP.

A Cheyenne Man Points Out the Defects in the Old Systems.

George Colangelo, the well known Italian watchman, is a pretty well posted man on dueling and in comparing the systems of swordsmanship of the various countries pointed out some interesting facts in connection with the Italian method.

The old world sword duel between the Italian count and the French prince seems to a bystander to add weight to the idea entertained for some time that Italy has the best system of swordsmanship exatnt. In 1893 an Italian named Pini, with some companions, exhibited his prowess with the foils in Chicago and other cities of the country. His tactics were a revelation to those who had been used to the more staid style of swordsmanship ,which is usually designated the French mode. This same Pini is probably the champion of Europe today, and the young Italian count who punctured the pride of Prince Henri of Orleans and the French with a groin thrust carried that master's tactics to the field.

The Italian school of swordsmanship appears to be as much superior to old styles as modern glove fighting is over obsolete London prize ring combat. It is more agility on the legs and, consequently, more momentum gotten for hitting, which principally mark the superiority of modern glove fighting over the old style. So with the Italian swordsman. He trains himself for leaping in and out and side-slipping quite as much as he has his arm and his eye. And having a mastery of such agility he naturally falls into feinting and trickery for an opening. The Italian master, Pini, was capable of making such lightning play with his steel and getting about with such rapidity to different positions of the fighting inclosure that, in boxing parlance, he was apt to make a monkey of an opponent.

SENATOR WARREN IN UTAH.

Speaks of the Prosperous Condition of the Cattle Industry.

The Salt Lake Tribune of recent date says:

"United States Senator Francis E. Warren of Wyoming is making a brief visit to the city. The precise nature of this business, Mr. Warren declines to tell, but it is said to relate to a big stock deal which the Wyoming senator is here to consummate.

"Stockmen in Wyoming are feeling unusually jubilant this year owing to a variety of reasons," said he last evening. "During the thirty years that I have been in the territory and state, the range has never been better. Stock of all kinds is sleek and in fine condition. Prices are good and promise to be even better. In consequence the cattlemen and the sheepmen are equally happy. Similar conditions obtain generally throughout the state so that there is a feeling of contentment everywhere, the stock business being so important an industry that its betterment affects all classes beneficially.

"Then the sale of the Union Pacific will have a good effect in the state generally as well as locally in the different cities along the line. Freedom from government control or supervision will give the new management, that purchases the property, an opportunity of serving the public solely and this without entanglements. It will be productive of other benefits as well.

"Everything seems to be shaped this year for the benefit of Wyoming. There is no boom, you understand. But conditions are steadily growing better and people believe that an era of prosperity is approaching."

"How about politics in Wyoming?" asked the reporter.

"There is nothing doing politically in the state. The first election to be held in the state will be that of a city council in Cheyenne on Jan. 1, and interest has not yet been awakened in it. It's the off-year and everyone is taking a rest."

"JUDGE" ALLEN TO WED.

The Well Known Rock Creek Resident to Be Married This Evening.

Dr. Rafter of Cheyenne, who has been spending a day in the city, left this morning for Medicine Bow, where he will this evening perform the happy ceremony uniting Judge Allen and Miss Schulte. The bride to be is a well known Cheyenne young lady.

The statement in the Boomerang yesterday was credulously received by those who are acquainted with Mr. Allen, for the fun-loving people along the line in this section have time and again announced the wedding of this gentleman and the majority thought the rumor at this time was the work of jesters. Mr. Allen and bride will leave Medicine Bow tonight for Salt Lake, and after spending a short time in that city will go to Cripple Creek, Colo., to reside.—Laramie Boomerang.

FOR SALE—A good Victor wheel, very cheap, at this office. Wm. C. Bartlett.

Just Received

A Complete Line of Men's DRESS and BUSINESS SUITS,

Varying in Price From $ 6 00 to $ 15.00

Also a complete line of Men's Pants from $1.00 to $5.00 a pair. For Real Bargains in Clothing or Furnishing Goods give us a call.

THE HUB

SHORT STORIES.

Picked Up by the Reporters in Their Daily Search for News.

Last night there was a force of men working in the Union Pacific machine shop.

The Sunday school picnic of the Congregational church was held today and a large number of young folks enjoyed the day in the country.

UNDER THE BED.

A Huge Rattlesnake Killed by J. M. Gilmore.

Mr. J. M. Gilmore, who has been working on a ranch near Horse creek came into town today and reports snakes in that section as very numerous. Mr. Gilmore was awakened recently by a rattling noise and getting up found a huge rattler under his bed. The reptile was immediately killed. Mr. Gilmore also killed a grey wolf on the way to town.

A DINING ROOM GIRL.

Wanted, at the Metropolitan hotel, a good dining room girl.

J. W. GRIFFIN.

WANTED—MALE HELP—Do you want a government position, $900 to $5,000 per annum? Pay sure. Work easy. Hours short. Life position. 30 to 60 days' annual leave with pay. We prepare by mail for high grade and appointment. Course of instruction, $5 to $12.50. Catalogue with details free. HUGHES' CIVIL SERVICE PREPARATION, Washington, D. C.

Beautiful eyes grow dull and dim
As the swift years steal away.
Beautiful, willowy forms so slim
Lose fairness with every day.
But she still is queen and hath charms to spare
Who wears youth's coronal—beautiful hair.

Preserve Your Hair

and you preserve your youth. "A woman is as old as she looks," says the world. No woman looks as old as she is if her hair has preserved its normal beauty. You can keep hair from falling out, restoring its normal color, or restore the normal color to gray or faded hair, by the use of

Ayer's Hair Vigor.

In Retrospect

Warren Richardson, Jr. was the first CFD chairman in 1897.

The Cheyenne Daily Sun-Leader.

VOL. XXX. —NO 299   CHEYENNE, WYOMING WEDNESDAY EVENING, SEPTEMBER 22, 1897.   PRICE FIVE CENTS

GRAND CELEBRATION
CHOICE CLOTHING

The autumn season is at hand and we are well prepared to meet it. Never before have we been prepared at so early a date with such a complete stock, embracing the world's choicest products.

We now invite every man and boy in need of a suit or overcoat to come and inspect our great stock.

Prompt concern will naturally share best.

M. MARKS.

WE HEAR OF SO MANY PEOPLE GOING TO KLONDIKE

WM. MYERS IS NOT GOING—HE IS SELLING WINTER UNDER-CLOTHING WHICH IS WELL WORTH WEARING THERE.

LOOK AT THESE PRICES—Gents' heavy knit underwear at 50 cents each
Gents' Fleece lined health underwear. Extra fine at $1, worth $1.25 each.
Gents' all wool natural underwear extra weight, worth $1.75, at $1.25 each.
Great Bargains in Ladies' Underwear.
50 dozen extra quality winter weight, fleeced, at 25c, worth 40c.
80 dozen extra quality heavy fleece Swiss ribbed, worth 65c, at 50c each.
Just received, Ladies' fine Swiss ribbed underwear, from 75c to $1.65 each.
Children's underwear at prices which CANNOT BE DUPLICATED.
Sizes ..16 18 20 22 24 26 28 30 32 34
Price 5 8 10 15 18 20 25 30 30 35
Children's fine silver ribbed:
Sizes ..16 18 20 22 24 26 28 30 32 34
Price ...10 15 18 20 25 30 35 40 45 45
REMEMBER THE ABOVE ARE SPECAL—COME WHLE THEY LAST.

WM. MYERS.

WAITING

For something to turn up is looking for the impossible to happen. The mountains of opportunity will not come to you. The grand variety in our selected stock of drugs, medicines, chemicals, patent medicines, fancy goods, novelties, toilet articles, perfumery, stationery, cutlery, combs, brushes, soaps and so many numerous odds and ends of new, attractive and useful th.ngs are in our store, and you must come here to get them.

We have paved the path to purchase with easy prices, but buyers must do the walking. Look most and oftenest. What's visible nowhere else, our stock is crowded with exclusive goods. Watch our grand holiday line, which will soon be in display.

Palace Pharmacy Drug Co.
A. R. Troxell, Ph. G. Manager
Graduate St. Louis College of Pharmacy.

THREE Shoemakers
in the day time and one at night all the time on hand at
A. HERMAN'S Shop

STILL RUSHING NORTH

LARG CAT

Lieut. For Tot

Seat Rosali other list th in the At V numb, who v try th kon. Ther naturi the Y H. Ha intent value and t The to St. river i protec arrivir east, i dall. for tl Humb North Tradi: north. Sche for Co ber ai There will b week Stea rive s ships arrive lameti Skagu

THE

PART ANI

Two I lies Okl. Wh Few

St. yellov seems tion f missi: amina declar sympt ragin; The of ago tal M ver n ernme ed in Cairo, clan i becan was t worki had l cases hospit case Healt was l get to and t city b resent regar "I tion c Deck: me in dinar yellov There symp kidne two tl sides, break has a tients "T! the I: yards came he cai "I antin charg tions. Tw. tities, the A! at M temp: been the y south: Dr. state matic to be dress

---

EVERYTHING IN READINESS

FOR THE FIRST FRONTIER DAY CELEBRATION IN WYOMING.

Which Will be the Most Successful Event in the State's History—Genuine and Interesting Races and Revival of Old Time Scenes—Some of the Day's Events.

One of the most interesting characters who will participate in the celebration of Frontier Day tomorrow is White Hawk, Jr., a very bright Indian of 46 years of age, who has passed through some interesting times and is the son of an Indian chief of no little fame, Standing Water, and is indirectly related to the famous Sitting Bull.

White Hawk was rather averse to conversation today, but finally condescended to give the reporter a few incidents in his early life and became enthusiastic and very sad at intervals when describing various circumstances in the early history of this country.

"It makes me feel badly to talk of olden times. The white man don't care for barren prairies and a life of hunting and fishing and camping," said he with a reflective twinkle, "but the Indian likes no other. It is like prison to put us in a city in close houses and all the inconveniences of what you call highly civilized life. Our fathers never lived that way and it isn't in our blood. You would feel abused if you were compelled to live in the mountains the whole year and make a living by killing buffaloes, bear and deer and wear their skins for clothes because your father didn't do that and it ain't in your blood. It is the same with the Indian. We are compelled to hide our nature and act as white folks, but it is not strange that occasionally our blood controls us and we seek our old life. You ask me about old times. You hurt me by that. Yes, I have been in battles with the white man. They came to our country and said all Indians are bad, and when we were seen the white men prepared for fight, and so we became the same way and said if white man is seen we fight. Some times white man beat us. They had good guns and plenty of shot. Indians were killed and we had to run away. White man killed all buffalo and wild animals until there is no more old times. Nearly all the Indians are at the happy hunting grounds. Yes, white man killed my father. I was a boy so high (about 12 years of age). White man was going to California and had lots of wagons and lots of white men. We had seven Indians and came around big mountain. White man shot my father and six Indians, but didn't shoot me. I lived with white man seventeen years, but city life is no good for Indian, so I come back."

White Hawk is a very entertaining talker and evidently has seen some hard times.

EARLY REMINISCENCES

ONE OF OUR OLD TIME CITIZENS RELATES EXCITING EVENTS OF EARLY DAYS.

Herman Haas Tells of Some Stirring Times Enacted in This Portion of Wyoming During the Sixties—Good Stories of Bad Men, Indians and

ATTRACTIONS ARRIVING.

Among the many interesting revivals of frontier scenes tomorrow will be old stage coach scenes and a typical coach used for twelve years in the Black Hills country arrived from the west today and was seen on our streets with four prancing steeds.

The program tomorrow will be all that could be desired. Entries to all the races are coming in in large numbers and this part of the program will be the best ever witnessed in the west. The hold-up scene and vigilantes and interference by the government troops was rehearsed today and will be a most exciting scene. The troops from Fort Russell will be camped in old time style at the fair grounds and each man will be provided with ten rounds of ammunition.

A sham battle will be an interesting event of the day. Capt. Pitcher has charge of this part of the program, which assures success.

The fair grounds will present a most picturesque appearance tomorrow and old time scenes will be exhibited with vividness.

Two bands will discourse music and admittance to the grounds is free.

The indications are that the city will be full of visitors from all directions.

BE SURE TO DECORATE.

Remember this is the inauguration of an annual state festival and everybody should decorate their homes and business houses. Make the town look bright and sociable. Let every individual see to it that the visitors receive very attention and carry pleasant memories of their visit to their homes. This is the day to celebrate and do it up in good shape.

Stage coach No. 2, with six horses, arrived from the west at 3 o'clock today. Cowboys are coming in in large numbers and already visitors are beginning to arrive from various directions. Everything is moving nicely and the grand success of the Frontier celebration is assured.

Trains will leave the depot for the fair grounds at 1 o'clock, 2 o'clock and 3 o'clock and will return after the races.

The janitors of the school buildings, churches and men in charge of engines are requested to ring bells and blow whistles and make all kinds of noise at high noon tomorrow.

A yoke of big oxen arrived at 3:30 this afternoon and are fine big animals. The Greeley band will arrive in Cheyenne at 12 o'clock and will discourse music during the day. The First Regiment band under Chas. Martin has rehearsed some fine new music and their program tomorrow will be well worth listening to. The city band will also play in the evening.

At 2 o'clock the first battalion of the Eighth United States infantry will appear upon the grounds and make camp, pitching their tents in picturesque form. After cowboy events are over there will be a skirmish drill, closing in a sham battle.

The officers in charge of the affair will be as follows: Commander in Chief, Capt. Pitcher; company E, Capt. Ames, Lieut. Simons; company F, Lieut. Langdon; company A, Lieut. Seyburn; company C, Capt. Hubert, Lieut. Merchant.

---

later on ran a barber shop here) and still another named DeBouvelle, had rooms at an old building which used to stand where the Hurd terrace now stands, in the west part of the city. I had my room there, and I also remember a party named Peters—yes, and some others, among whom was a Swede, whose name I can't recall. It transpired one morning that during then light somebody got away with $800 belonging to the Swede, and there was a great stir about it, of that evening I came down in to witness the conclusion ing match, which took place building, a sort of theater, od then about opposite ston Taylor's place stands am a little ahead of my story should have explained that e day Grier Beaucaire and e had been arrested for getr with the Swede's money, if and four others had signonds. Well, as I was saythe walking match was ent home, but here I found pon barred, and finally Pee in, and I saw that he was atty nearly to death. I asknat was up, and he explained at the vigilance committee there and taken these three y with them. I made up that it was about time for looking out, as I was on ds. Perhaps these fellows after me, so I slipped down S. marshal's office and found y marshal and related what ened. He said that there ing he could do about it, at home, but before daylight men returned, but wouldn't

The meetings were held in the spalace and during rt to the le great Vestminhe archand the 1 at St. ning of shop of shops in ve funcepressed which a bearing a church n of the s issued deast to rld.) Talbot churchcekdays. thedral, number rches in ominent He only, de- of the gentry via gave ps were r royal opporPrincess Duchess

Niagara op Talladstone man reing them, uch that ee them ica. For f a very ny quesd showand a nature. simply lot; "he ditions they are ell low, in tariff ondon it the Unin great cussions Ameri- of the and in n of the erchants celented over the with a and re e that it coming thedral cal bur-

STMASTER APPOINTED. ington, Sept. 21.—W. E. Taylor day appointed postmaster at :a, Big Horn county, vice John n, removed.

THE BISHOP IS HOME

A PLEASANT AND PROFITABLE VISIT TO THE OLD WORLD.

Something in Relation to the Conference at Lambeth Palace—A Visit to the Grand Old Man—Mr. Gladstone Expresses Friendship for America—Improved Conditions.

Bishop Talbot returned this morning from his trip to the old world, where he was in attendance upon the conference of bishops, held in Guild hall of Lambeth palace, London. The bishop is looking hale and hearty and says that he enjoyed the vacation from his mission work to the utmost, although it was work from the time he left his See City till his return.

It is the custom of the archbishop of Canterbury to call together every ten years the bishops of the church. For this action custom is the only authority which the archbishop possesses as bishops are all of equal rank and station. This deference is shown him on account of the fact that his is the oldest diocese in the kingdom of Great Britain. There were in attendance 190 bishops, from all sections of the globe, Africa, Australia, America, China, India, Japan and elsewhere. There were three negro bishops from Africa present. In other countries, the church is known by different names. In this country it is the Episcopal church, in England it is the Church of England, etc., but its objects and fundamental principles are the same the world around.

TO THE FAIR GROUNDS
Special trains will run to the fair grounds tomorrow afternoon, leaving the Union Pacific depot at 1, 2 and 3 o'clock.

FRONTIER DAY.

Union Pacific Places on Sale Tickets for the Event Thursday.

Traveling Passenger Agent Angler of the Union Pacific returned this morning from aiding in completing the Frontier Day program at Cheyenne.

Invitations have been received by Mayor McMurray and the city council, the chamber of commerce, the mining exchange, the president and directors of the Festival of Mountain and Plain, the Denver Athletic, Denver, Calumet, Lotus, Denver Wheel and Arapahoe Wheel clubs, and accepted. The advance sale of tickets began yesterday at the Union Pacific and other railroad offices, two days earlier than ever noted before in the history of Denver ticket offices.

The Cheyenne papers recently advertised for "a man wanted—to hang." The Post copied it. It referred to a thrilling frontier scene to be introduced of a lynching and rescue of the victim by United States troops from Fort Russell. A man came into the Union Pacific office this morning and exclaimed: "I just as soon hang as not if I could get there. Give me transportation." The transportation was forthcoming.

TICKETS FOR GRAND STAND.

At the request of a number of citizens, the Frontier Day committee have decided to sell a limited number (not over 500) of tickets for seats in grand stand. They can be obtained at Palace Pharmacy drug store from 9 a. m. to 11 a. m. Secure your tickets and avoid the rush at the fair grounds.

uainted with the vigilantes and ith me, so that we understood ther after that."

AT THE HUB.
Ladies' Fleece-lined Vests and winter weight, at 25 cents each. 40 cents.

your Overcoats and Suits at b, and get the best for the least

---

Royal makes the food pure, wholesome and delicious.

ROYAL BAKING POWDER Absolutely Pure

ROYAL BAKING POWDER CO., NEW YORK.

BROTHERS QUARREL

CHARLES AND AL ROGERS HAVE AN ALTERCATION.

In Which Both Men are Badly Injured — Police Itnerfered Before Either Man was Dangerously Wounded.

Citizens in the vicinity of Roger's blacksmith shop were called to that place this morning by calls from a crowd that had been attracted by a fight between Charles Rogers, the well-known blacksmith, and his brother, Al Rogers, who formerly resided in this city, but who has spent the last few years as a miner in Colorado. From what information can be gleaned, it appears that Al Rogers is a dissipated man of vicious habits, and attacked his brother on account of his refusal to divide the Rogers property, a half of which Al claims he is entitled to. The cause of the final fight is not further known.

Al Rogers hit his brother with a bar of iron over the head and on the arm, inflicting ugly wounds. In defending himself Charles dealt Al a blow over the head with a bar of iron. The interference of the police at this point averted further trouble. Both men are badly hurt, but it is thought and hoped that neither is dangerously wounded.

TONIGHT! TONIGHT!
THE TURNER BALL TAKES PLACE TONIGHT. DANC NG BEGINS PROMPTLY AT 9 O'CLOCK. NAPRESTKE'S FULL ORCHESTRA WILL FURNISH THE MUSIC. THERE WILL BE A FINE DANCE PROGRAM AND SEVERAL EXTAS.

FOR RENT—Seven room house, 1915 House street, two blocks east of Central school. H. B. Patten.

Men's Fall Underwear at 45c each, worth 75c.
THE HUB.

TAX LEVY LESS.
State Examiner Henderson stated to a reporter this morning that the general tax levy throughout the state is less this year than ever before. Along the Union Pacific the only county the levy of which for general county purposes will exceed 9 1-2 mills is Uinta county. This is a very encouraging state of affairs when past conditions are considered.

FOR RENT—Offices, houses and furnished and unfurnished rooms. Will quote very low figures. Apply to J.

Our I's and.... ....Other Eyes.

Our I's are just as strong as they were fifty years ago, when we hear of a number of them. But we have less and less cause to praise ourselves, since others do the praising, and we are more than willing for you to see us through other eyes. This is how we look to S. F. Boyce, wholesale and retail druggist, Duluth, Minn, who after a quarter of a century of observation writes:

"I have sold Ayer's Sarsaparilla for more than 25 years, both at wholesale and retail, and have never heard anything but words of praise from my customers; not a single complaint has ever reached me. I believe Ayer's Sarsaparilla to be the best blood purifier, that has been introduced to the general public." This, from a man who has sold thousands of dozens of Ayer's Sarsaparilla, is strong testimony. But it only echoes popular sentiment the world over, which has, "Nothing but words of praise for Ayer's Sarsaparilla."

Any doubt about it? Send for "Curebook" It tells doubts and cures doubters. Address J. C. AYER CO., Lowell, Mass.

Men's Wool Suits at $4.95 and up at THE HUB. Get one and compare with others at $8.

200 pairs Ladies' Fine Shoes at $1.80, former price $3, all this season's styles. Get a pair. It's like finding them.
THE HUB.

For first-class goods at popular prices visit THE HUB. It pays.

New Millinery goods now on sale at THE HUB.

Rudy Hoffman, was CFD chairman in 1946 (50th Anniversary Year).

Hoffman's daughter, Lois, was Miss Frontier the same year (1946).

CHEYENNE	PROGRAM
July 26, 27, 28 and 29 1921	Third and Fourth Days July 28th and 29th

CHEYENNE'S
Silver Anniversary and Twenty-Fifth Annual
FRONTIER DAYS

OFFICIAL PROGRAM

Third Day, July 28th

Track Event No. 1—Barrel Race. Purse $75, divided $35, $25, $15.

Track Event No. 2—Rope and Change Race. Purse $75, divided $35, $25, $15.

Track Event No. 3—Men's half-mile Cowpony Race. Purse $75 each day, divided $40, $25, $10. Regulation cow horse saddles to be used.

Field Event No. 4—Ladies' World's Championship Bucking Contest. Purse $200, divided $75 and $200 Brunswick Phonograph, presented by Brandeis Stores of Omaha, Nebraska, Second $60; Third $40; Fourth $25.

Track Event No. 5—Cowboy's Stake Race. Purse $50, divided $25, $15, $10.

Track Event No. 6—One quarter mile free for all race for Officers 15th U. S. Cavalry, Fort D. A. Russell. Officers to ride own entries. Purse $50 divided $25, $15, $10.

Track Event No. 7—Roman Race, Free for All. Purse $100, divided $60, $25, $15.

Track Event No. 8—Indian Relay Race, one and one-half miles. Purse $50, divided $25, $15, $10.

Track Event No. 9—World's Championship Trick and Fancy Riding Contest. Purse $200, divided $75 and $300 saddle presented by Miss Pauline Frederick, Goldwyn Studios, Los Angeles; $60, $40, $25. Contestants to perform each day.

Track Event No. 10—Rep Race. Purse $50, divided $25, $15, $10.

Field Event No. 11—Cow Boy's Bucking Contest. Purse $1500, divided final money, first $700 and $500 saddle presented by Mr. Carl R. Gray, President of the Union Pacific Railroad; Second $300; Third $200. Day money three days, $50, $30, $20. Entrance fee $25. Frontier Committee to furnish all saddles to be used in this event. No outside saddles will be allowed in this event.

Track Event No. 12—Cowgirls one-half mile Cowpony Race. Purse $75, divided $40, $25, $10. Conditions same as men's.

Track Event No. 13—Indian War Dance.

Track Event No. 14—Cowgirls Championship Denver Post Relay Race, one and one-half miles. Purse $1200 $300 each day divided $175, $75, $50.

Field Event No. 15—Calf Roping Contest. Entrance Fee $20. Purse $800. Final money to be $250, $150, $50. Day money for three days $50, $30, $20. Half of entrance fee money to be added to day money purse and divided accordingly. Stetson hat presented to winner by Daiber Clothing Co., Cheyenne, Wyoming. Fastest time one calf $50.

Track Event No. 16—Indian Squaw Race. Purse $15, divided $7.50, $5, $2.50.

Track Event No. 17—Men's Relay Race. Purse, $1200, $300 each day, divided $175, $75, $50. One and one-half miles.

Track Event No. 18—Trick Roping Contest. Purse $300, divided $150, $75, $50, $25. Contestants to perform each day. Pair of boots from Connelly & Meyer to winner.

Track Event No. 19—Steer Bulldogging Contest. Purse $1000, divided final money $350, $200, $100, pair of boots from Shepard & Klett. Day money three days, first $50, $30, $20. Entrance fee $20. half to be added to day money purse and divided accordingly. Fastest time one steer, $50.

Field Event No. 20—Steer Roping Contest, tie down. Purse $1500. Final money $700, $300, $150, day money three days $50, $30, $20. Entrance fee $25. Fastest time one steer $50. Pair of boots from Bon Shoe & Clothing Co. to winner.

Field Event No. 21—Bare Back Riding.

Field Event No. 22—Wild Steer Riding.

Track Event No. 23—Indian Buck Race. Purse $15 divided $7.50, $5, $2.50.

Track Event No. 24—Wild Horse Race. Purse $800, $200 each day, divided $100, $50, $35, $15. Entrance fee $5. Fourteen men to ride each day.

Fourth Day, July 29th

Track Event No. 1—Barrel Race. Purse, $75, divided $35, $25, $15.

Track Event No. 2—Rope and Change Race. Purse $75, divided $35, $25, $15.

Track Event No. 3—Cowgirls Stake Race. Purse $50, divided $25, $15, $10. One hundred yards to line and back.

Field Event No. 4—Ladies Championship Bucking Contest finals. Purse $200. Divided $75, and $200 Brunswick Phonograph, presented by the Brandeis Stores, Omaha, Nebraska. $60, $40, $25.

Track Event No. 5—One-half mile Free for All Race for Officers of the 15th U. S. Cavalry, Fort D. A. Russell. Officers to ride their own entries. Purse $50, divided $25, $15, $10. Army blanket from Hedgcock & Jones, Denver, to winner.

Track Event No. 6—Roman Standing Race. Purse $100, divided $60, $25, $15.

Track Event No. 7—World's Championship Trick and Fancy Riding Contest finals. Purse $200, divided $75 and $300 saddle presented by Miss Pauline Frederick, Goldwyn Studios, Los Angeles, $60, $40, $25. Contestants to perform each day.

Track Event No. 8—Indian Relay Race, one and one-half miles. Purse $50, divided $25, $15, $10.

Track Event No. 9—Cowgirls one-half mile Cowpony Race. Purse $75, divided $40, $25, $10. Free for all. Regulation cow horse saddles to be used.

Track Event No. 10—Rep Race. Purse $50, divided $25, $15, $10.

Track Event No. 11—Cowboys one-half mile Cowpony Race. Purse $75, divided $40, $25, $10. Regulation cow horse saddles to be used.

Field Event No. 12—Cow Boys Bucking Contest. Purse $1500, divided final money, $700, and $500 saddle presented by Mr. Carl R. Gray, President of the Union Pacific Railroad, $300, and $200. Frontier Committee to furnish all saddles to be used in this event. No outside saddles to be allowed.

Track Event No. 13—Cowgirl's Championship Denver Post Relay Race, one and one-half miles. Purse $1200, $300 each day, divided $175, $75, $50.

Track Event No. 14—Indian War Dance.

Field Event No. 15—Calf Roping Contest. Entrance fee $20. Purse $800. Final money to be $250, $150, $50.

Track Event No. 16—Indian Squaw Race. Purse $15, divided $7.50, $5, $2.50.

Track Event No. 17—Men's Relay Race. Purse $1200, $300 each day divided $175, $75, $50. Winner of most heats to be presented with Stetson hat by Gano-Downs Clothing Company, Denver, Colorado.

Track Event No. 18—Trick Roping Contest. Purse $300, divided $150, $75, $50, $25. Pair of boots from Connelly & Meyer to winner.

Track Event No. 19—Steer Bulldogging Contest finals. Purse $1000, divided final money $350, $200, $100, pair of boots from Shepard & Klett. Entrance fee $20.

Field Event No. 20—Steer Roping Contest, tie down. Purse $1500, final money $700, $300, $200. Fastest time one steer $50. Pair of boots from Bon Shoe & Clothing Co. to winner.

Field Event No. 21—Bare Back Riding.

Field Event No. 22—Steer Riding.

Track Event No. 23—Indian Buck Race. Purse $15, divided $7.50, $5, $2.50.

Track Event No. 24—Wild Horse Race. Purse $800, $200 each day divided $100, $50, $35, $15. Entrance fee $5. Fourteen men to ride each day.

The McAlpin Hotel, of New York City, New York, are awarding a beautiful solid gold, diamond studded Trophy, to the World's Champion all around Cowgirl.
MANY OTHER SPECIAL PRIZES YET TO BE AWARDED.
This program subject to change by Committee, without notice.
Three big night shows, commencing eight o clock sharp, July 26, 27, 28. Many special features.
Big athletic entertainment at Fort D. A. Russell, night of July 29.

ARENA DIRECTORS
F. D. BOICE
C. W. HIRSIG
Address all Communications, Frontier Days Committee, Cheyenne, Wyo.

Military Maneuvers Each Day By Detachment Troops 15th Cavalry Fort D. A. Russell and Other Thrilling Military Features

Wyoming State Tribune, July 23, 1921. Silver Anniversary Program.

Lorena Trickey, world's champion all around woman rider, and holder of the famous McAlpin Trophy, who will defend her title at the Silver Anniversary Frontier Days. The winner will take the gold, silver and diamond plaque for 1921 as a permanent prize, and is also brought to New York as the guest of the McAlpin Hotel, to receive it.

Wyoming State Tribune, July 27, 1921.

All Dolled Up For The Big Show

Wyoming State Tribune, July 26, 1921.

RIDE 'IM, BRONCHO!

Wyoming State Tribune, July 27, 1921.

Mary and Joseph Adragna
Bess Arnold
Beverly Aylward
Cara Baber
Lorraine Backus
Joyce Bailey
Joann Baird
Louise Holmes Bartlett
Valerie Bastian
Mr. & Mrs. Palmer Black
Loretta Boucher
William F. Boyd
Mike Brown
Yvonne Busing
Marvin Chavoya
Alex Connell
Andrea Cook
Carol Drake Crump
Jennifer DeKock
Linda & Mark Detweiler
William & Marietta Dinneen
Ellen Downs
Jean Nimmo Dubois
Brian Dunlop
Rita Edwards
Berniece Farris
Christine Lummis Ferguson
Shirley Flynn
Ed Fowler
Bernadine "Bernie" Furman
Barney Grandpre
Carl Halladay, Jr.
Ila Hanson
Frances Hardy
Mary Lou Harrington
Jean & Paul Hickey
Beverly Holmes
Al Huffman
Jim Hunnicutt
Lilo Jessup
Gertrude Johnson
Robert Johnson
Stan Kepley
Mike Keys
Ronda Kolinske
Jim Lynch
Marvel McCraken
Robin McIntosh

Janet Deaver McLean
Beth Miller
Priscilla Miller
Margaret Mohrlang
Richard Morse
Ned Murray
Bill Nation
Wayne Neeman
N. Walt Nelson
Mary Ann G. Neuman
John & Ramona Niland
Alan O'Hashi
Carla Painter
Juanita Patterson
Mr. & Mrs. Robert Pearson
Juanita Pennington
"Stovepipe" Pette
Judy Pixley
Sheryl Powers
Robert Pulse
Paulette Rasmussen
B. J. Richardson
Dorothy Richardson
Phil Richardson
LouElla N. Ross
Harold "Hal" Russell
Jim Russell
John & Fern Sapienza
Anna Sherman
Amy Smith
Ann Dinneen Smith
Rose Smith
Eve Souply
Norman Stark
Charlene Stogsdill
Darlene Tate
Enola Thomas
Beriah "Bill" Thompson
Julia Todd
Beverly Vandehei
Randy Wagner
Bob Walston
Cheryl Webster
Janice "Jan" Wiejek
Virginia Wiese
Margy Wilson
Old West Museum

Looking To The Future...

Your Favorite Photos Here

Your Favorite Photos Here